NAZI HUNGER POLITICS

Rowman & Littlefield Studies in Food and Gastronomy

Food studies is a vibrant and thriving field encompassing not only cooking and eating habits but also issues such as health, sustainability, food safety, and animal rights. Scholars in disciplines as diverse as history, anthropology, sociology, literature, and the arts focus on food. The mission of **Rowman & Littlefield Studies in Food and Gastronomy** is to publish the best in food scholarship, harnessing the energy, ideas, and creativity of a wide array of food writers today. This broad line of food-related titles will range from food history, interdisciplinary food studies monographs, general interest series, and popular trade titles to textbooks for students and budding chefs, scholarly cookbooks, and reference works.

Titles in the Series

Appetites and Aspirations in Vietnam: Food and Drink in the Long Nineteenth Century, by Erica J. Peters
Three World Cuisines: Italian, Mexican, Chinese, by Ken Albala
Food and Social Media: You Are What You Tweet, by Signe Rousseau
Food and the Novel in Nineteenth-Century America, by Mark McWilliams
Man Bites Dog: Hot Dog Culture in America, by Bruce Kraig and Patty Carrol
New Orleans: A Food Biography, by Elizabeth M. Williams (Big City Food Biographies series)
A Year in Food and Beer: Recipes and Beer Pairings for Every Season, by Emily Baime and Darin Michaels
Breakfast: A History, by Heather Arndt Anderson (The Meals series)
Celebraciones Mexicanas: History, Traditions, and Recipes, by Andrea Lawson Gray and Adriana Almazán Lahl
Food History Almanac: Over 1,300 Years of World Culinary History, Culture, and Social Influence, by Janet Clarkson
The Food Section: Newspaper Women and the Culinary Community, by Kimberly Wilmot Voss
Small Batch: Pickles, Cheese, Chocolate, Spirits, and the Return of Artisanal Foods, by Suzanne Cope
Nazi Hunger Politics: A History of Food in the Third Reich, by Gesine Gerhard

NAZI HUNGER POLITICS

A History of Food in the Third Reich

Gesine Gerhard

ROWMAN & LITTLEFIELD
Lanham • Boulder • New York • London

Published by Rowman & Littlefield
A wholly owned subsidiary of The Rowman & Littlefield Publishing Group, Inc.
4501 Forbes Boulevard, Suite 200, Lanham, Maryland 20706
www.rowman.com

Unit A, Whitacre Mews, 26-34 Stannary Street, London SE11 4AB

British Library Cataloguing in Publication Information Available

Library of Congress Cataloging-in-Publication Data

Gerhard, Gesine, 1969–
Nazi hunger politics : a history of food in the Third Reich / Gesine Gerhard.
pages cm. —(Rowman & Littlefield studies in food and gastronomy)
Includes bibliographical references and index.
ISBN 978-1-4422-2724-8 (cloth : alkaline paper) — ISBN 978-1-4422-2725-5 (ebook) 1. Food supply—Government policy—Germany—History—20th century. 2. National socialism—Social aspects. 3. World War, 1939–1945—Food supply—Germany. 4. Food—Political aspects—Germany—History—20th century. 5. Food—Social aspects—Germany—History—20th century. 6. Food—Symbolic aspects—Germany—History—20th century. 7. Hunger—Political aspects—Germany—History—20th century. 8. Hunger—Social aspects—Germany—History—20th century. 9. Germany—Politics and government—1933–1945. 10. Germany—Social conditions—1933–1945. I. Title.
HD9015.G32G37 2015
363.8'56094309043—dc23

2015005789

∞ ™ The paper used in this publication meets the minimum requirements of American National Standard for Information Sciences Permanence of Paper for Printed Library Materials, ANSI/NISO Z39.48-1992.

Printed in the United States of America

CONTENTS

LIST OF ILLUSTRATIONS

ACKNOWLEDGMENTS

This book has been in the works for several years, and along the way, I have received support from many people. I will always be grateful for the encouragement, the critical feedback, and the distractions that helped me continue my labors. The research started in the Federal Archives in Koblenz, Germany, a most welcoming place for any historian. Gregor Pickro in Koblenz represents one of the many archivists I could reliably count on. Herr Pickro suggested I contact the Backe family, and reading this book, you will know where this led me. David Schoenbaum deserves credit as my mentor early on, for it was his critical eye that pushed me much further than I thought I could go. I also owe a large debt to my students at the University of the Pacific, whose curiosity is a constant source of energy. My colleagues in the history department and beyond have been wonderful and inspirational. A special thank-you goes to Ken Albala, who introduced me to food studies and has been supportive since I first put foot on this campus almost sixteen years ago. Caroline Cox gave feedback on everything I needed to talk about, and only her untimely death in July 2014 prevented her from reading drafts of all chapters. The weekly phone calls with Edie Sparks kept me on target during the last writing phase when deadlines could not be pushed out any further. Bill Swagerty and Robin Imhof allowed me to nag them with questions I had along the way. Thank you to Mike Sharp for his careful copyediting of the manuscript and to Gerda Story, who transcribed Ursula Backe's diaries for me. I am indebted as well to Wendi Schnaufer, the editor at the press who first recruited me. She had great ideas and a vision for this project. Thank you to peer reviewers of chapter drafts at any stage—especially Ernst Langthaler, Andreas Agoçs, Ute Gerhard, Wendi Schnaufer, Ken Albala, and Greg Rohlf—the book would not be the same without their comments.

I would also like to thank the Backe siblings, who generously met with me, answered my questions, and allowed me to use their mother's diaries, even though they worried that my work would cast their father in a new light. I am grateful for the friends I have made in California, who have been essential to balance life and work, and for the old friends who stayed in touch over the years. I am lucky to have two sisters, Nele and Ulrike, who will always remain close, no matter how many thousands of miles are between us. The phone conversations with my twin sister kept me going and encouraged me when I needed it most. I would like to thank my mom as well, who has served as a role model for me since I was little, and my dad, too, for his relentless enthusiasm for everything I do. Last but not least I want to thank my husband, Greg, for all the delicious meals he cooks for us with so much love, and our three children, Konrad, Marlene and Charlotte, for all they give and take. It is to them and other little picky eaters that this book is dedicated.

INTRODUCTION

MEETING THE BACKE FAMILY

As the train comes closer and closer to Hanover, I watch the characteristic North German landscape racing past my window. My eyes register the constantly changing scenery as picturesque small towns give way to the green fields and thick forests with the Harz Mountains always visible in the distance. The train crosses rivers and valleys and accelerates in open spaces. Everything is muted. For my homesick North German heart, still not used to taking the car wherever I have to go, there seems to be nothing more relaxing than taking the train in Germany. It feels so luxurious to sit in the fast ICE train transporting me without any apparent effort from one city to the next. I have time to read, work on my laptop, or simply look out the window and let my thoughts wander. My mind often turns to the task awaiting me in Hanover, for it is there that I will personally meet with the children of Herbert Backe, the second Reich Minister of Food and Agriculture during the Nazi period, a central figure in my research for years. Backe was in charge of food politics during the Third Reich and the brain behind the notorious *Hungerplan* ("hunger plan"), a plan that foresaw the starvation of millions of Soviet citizens during World War II. What would I say to his children? How would they receive me, a historian who might uncover truths about their father that would tarnish the memory they had protected for so many decades?

In postwar German historiography, Herbert Backe had received little attention thus far. He had killed himself in his prison cell in Nuremberg before he was tried by the American Military Tribunal, and his name had been forgotten. His boss of many years, Reich Minister of Food and Agriculture Richard Walther Darré, on the other hand, had survived to face trial and was condemned to seven years in prison as a Nazi perpetrator. Backe's own crucial role in the murderous plans for the economic exploitation of the Soviet Union had only recently been unearthed.

When he committed suicide in April 1947, Backe left behind a wife and four teenage children. The oldest daughter, Armgard, was born in 1932 followed by Albrecht (1933), Arnulf (1934), and Arnd (1936). Three of them still live in Hanover, not far from the place the Backes had called home in the 1920s and 1930s. I was meeting the siblings, now in their seventies, and planned to ask them for permission to read their mother's diaries. Ursula Backe had written a diary from 1927 to 1947 and had given the five notebooks filled with her handwriting to the Federal Archives (*Bundesarchiv*) in Koblenz. The personal collection of Herbert Backe in the archives also contained letters and other documents. The diaries were still under an edict of "restricted access" (*Sperrfrist*) and could not be read by anybody without the Backe family's special permission. Gregor Pickro, a helpful archivist in Koblenz, suggested that I contact the Backes directly. He provided me with their home address and during my four-week stay in Koblenz I had sent a letter to the Backe children.

The Backes' answer to my request had been noncommittal. They asked to meet with me first before giving me permission to read the diaries. So here I was, on the train to Hanover, preparing for my first conversation with the children of someone I believed to be a Nazi perpetrator. I was nervous. As a historian, all the human subjects I had studied thus far had been deceased. I had never held any oral history interviews or professionally interacted much with witnesses. All the primary sources I had used could be found in archives and private collections. This task was different. I was going to meet the children of my historical subject and I needed their approval. I wanted something from them. What would I say if they asked me what I intended to do with the diaries? Was I not going to use the information to prove that their father was indeed a Nazi ideologist with little sympathy for Russian people? How would I feel if I were in their situation? What if the conversation turned out to be really awkward?

At the train station in Hanover, I bought a bouquet of flowers and took a taxi to the address that I had been given. Ten minutes later I apprehensively walked into the little townhouse. To my surprise, I felt immediately at ease. This place looked a lot like my parents' living room! The interior had the characteristic layout of a house in North Germany, the coffee table set with tablecloth, fine china, and hot tea, and I could not help but say out loud that this felt like home. After this unscripted comment, our conversation went smoothly. I would not describe the atmosphere as particularly warm, but it was friendly and cooperative. The Backe children wanted to know what I was going to do with the information from the diaries, and they shared their concerns that the reputation of their father had to be protected. I quickly understood that the family did not want their cherished memories of him to be tarnished.

In the Backes' living room I did not make any promises about how I would portray their father in my work. They acknowledged that they wanted to find out more about his political role, but felt that the "truth" was often misrepresented in publications or in the media. I promised that I would keep their concerns in mind. After a few hours and several cups of tea, I said my good-byes. I went to the Hotel Grübchen in Hanover, where I would stay overnight. When I came back from dinner, the receptionist handed me a letter from Armgard Henning, née Backe. In the letter, Armgard gave me written permission to read and use the diaries of Ursula Backe, following the rules of the Federal Archives (*Bundesarchiv*).

Letter in hand, I went straight back to the archives the following day. The helpful archivist Gregor Pickro was just as enthusiastic as I was about the permission and quickly brought me the original diaries. There were five little notebooks, every page filled with Ursula's handwriting. I sat down at my desk near the big window overlooking the courtyard of the archives and opened the first page to start reading. I was shocked to find that I could not decipher a word! I had seen my share of old handwriting and had learned the basic rules of how to recognize letters, but this looked different. Never had it occurred to me that Ursula Backe would write in *Sütterlin*, a style of German handwriting taught in German schools for a short period in the 1920s and early 1930s.[1] Ursula Backe continued to use *Sütterlin* at least in private communications—and in her diaries.

My initial excitement soon gave way to frustration, since I could hardly make sense of any sentences on any given page. I had only about ten days left to work in the archives before I would fly home. How was I to accomplish what I had set out to do? The next day, I came back with a cheat sheet that helped me recognize letters, but after a few hours I was only able to decipher single words and could still not understand whole sentences. The archivist suggested that I make photocopies and read the material at home where I would not have to worry about time. With a suitcase full of photocopies, I returned to California where I spent the next six months learning *Sütterlin* and slowly making my way through the diaries. At this point I was fortunate to make the acquaintance of Gerda Story, a native German and retired teacher in the Bay Area who was teaching German classes at the University of the Pacific. She had earlier learned to write in the *Sütterlin* script and later in her life continued to work with it. I hired Ms. Story to transcribe the complete diaries. She turned out to be the perfect person for the job since her historical curiosity and semantic sensitivity guided her transcriptions of even the most obscure individual words, even the names of remote places—no matter how illegible the original was. By the end of the year, I had a document with the transcription of all five diaries.

In the years to come I would use this document to study Herbert Backe's food politics and to understand the man behind the politics. When I wrote and talked about him at history conferences, the conversations with the Backe family were always on my mind. I can't deny that meeting the Backe children has affected the way I think about him, and has sometimes influenced how I write about him. The subject of my study had taken on a very real and human shape and was closer to me than I could have imagined. More specifically, I could not help but think how Armgard, Arnd, and Albrecht (I never met the third brother who lived in Berlin) would react when they read my work.

During my second visit with the Backes a couple of years later (December 2007), I asked them how it felt to be the children of a Nazi perpetrator and quickly realized that the question had really surprised them. They had never thought of their father as a war criminal! He had been in charge of food during the war, and yes, German stomachs came before Russian stomachs—but would not all responsible politicians have acted the same way? I pushed a little further, and asked them how they felt after their father committed suicide and how they talked about their father with family members and friends. Armgard explained that other people around her rarely mentioned her father and his politics. She remembered that only once years later a former classmate had asked her if there *was* anything about her father during the Nazi period. In Germany in the 1950s, the plight of the Backe family did not stand out. Many families had lost fathers, brothers, or sons in the war. Loved ones had died at the front or were missing or wounded. Many had been prisoners of war and if they returned months or years later, they never talked about the suffering they had experienced. In that sense, the Backes were like innumerable other German families. They cherished the memories of their late father, but never really confronted questions of responsibility or guilt.[2]

Over the years, Backe's widow Ursula had been the steward of ways in which her husband was remembered. She had carefully collected every document and had clipped out newspaper articles that mentioned him. She had organized his papers and handed many of them over to the Federal Archives in Koblenz.[3] She even transcribed and typed some of her husband's handwritten documents—like the *Grosser Bericht*, a sort of political testament that Backe wrote in the Nuremberg prison while awaiting his trial. She was a conscientious caretaker of records and events, a characteristic also often evident in the diaries she had written for almost two decades, from the beginning of her husband's meteoric political career to its final collapse in 1947. The diaries were the reason I was sitting in the living room of the Backe children. Excerpts had become public, but no other historian had read them in their entirety. At this point in time, I had no idea how valuable these handwritten documents would be as a historical source. Backe's wife had recorded in detail daily events of her husband's political life, his thoughts and frustrations. She also wrote about personal matters like the births of her four children, their first steps and words. These topics that are the substance of any diary, however, clearly played a minor role in Ursula's diaries. She had posterity in mind when she sat down, sometimes daily, to write her notes. She wrote with a strong historical consciousness of the magnitude of events occurring around her, events that needed to be recorded.

CONFRONTING THE PAST: A WORD ABOUT THE SOURCES

Personal documents such as diaries and letters can be tricky historical sources and have to be interpreted with much care. Ursula Backe's notebooks were a unique discovery. She had written with a keen historical sense about things she felt would be remembered in the distant future, even if not everybody recognized their significance at the time she lived and wrote. Her ideological convictions led her to an almost unconditional support of the Nazi cause, but it was probably more than simply ideological fervor that drove her to record her thoughts. A close observer of politics herself, she wrote about meetings between her husband and Darré, for example, with an eye for detail and perspective that goes beyond the mere chronicling of events. She used direct quotes by her husband from their conversations and commented on his reaction to his meetings or exchanges.

In addition to the diaries, there are many personal letters in the Backe collection in the *Bundesarchiv*. Just like his wife, Herbert himself was an active letter writer and he described in detail his daily struggles, his frustration with his job and colleagues (especially Darré). He often reflected on his personal motivations and attempted to explore in writing his most fundamental convictions. In the many letters written by Backe to his wife over the years, he talked both objectively about the political situation but also about his personal perspective toward political affairs and colleagues. The letters shed light on a mind with an unusual capacity for a thorough analysis of the people around him. All together, the many pages Ursula filled over the years and the letters provide an intimate portrayal of the man who was in charge of food policy and, ultimately, the mass starvation in the occupied territories.

The diaries led me to explore another dimension of the story. The meetings with Backe's children and the follow-up e-mails made clear that they took the business of guarding their father's memory seriously. It became an interesting case study in understanding how a family dealt with the memory of a loved one who had been part of the murderous Nazi regime. At the beginning of the twenty-first century, a great number of books written by the second and third postwar generation are being published. After decades of silence, children and grandchildren of victims and perpetrators seem to feel the need to address their family's legacy and to tell the public about it—and the public is eager to learn.[4] The Backes seemed to worry about changes in the public image of their father that could come with the new scrutiny. Ursula Backe had strongly supported Herbert and shared his convictions during the Third Reich. The question arises how, on her own, she had dealt with the collapse of the Nazi regime, the lost war, and Herbert's imprisonment and suicide in 1947. He was the father of her four children and had advised her—in a worst-case scenario—to end their lives since a world without National Socialism was a world without value and meaning. He was not at her side to confront the defeat and the difficult postwar years. The lease for the farm in Hornsen, not far from Hanover, that had been the family's home since the late 1920s, expired in 1948. Ursula received some compensation for the valuables on the farm, and this allowed her to raise her family without her husband's income.[5] More questions arise about Ursula's relationship with her children concerning their father's memory. How did she talk to them about him and what did she want them to remember? How did the children grow up and deal with the loss of their father? Since Herbert took his life before the trial, which without a doubt would have put his name on the record as a war criminal and a Nazi perpetrator, the family never had to think of him in those terms.

Sixty years later, it still seemed hard for the Backe children to confront any issues of their father's guilt or responsibility. In our conversations, the words "misinterpretation" and "misunderstanding" came up more than once, and they still view their father's policies as well meaning. Their general attitude is: "Germans at home had to be fed first, that was his job." More importantly, all statements were made with great care and only after checking in with the other siblings. The privacy of the family was also carefully guarded. When I asked the siblings if I could talk with their children about how they remembered their grandfather, I was told that that would go too far. I therefore did not investigate this angle much further with the Backes.

I am very grateful for the information the Backe family has shared. Ursula Backe—who passed away in the 1990s—kept records throughout her long life of anything that was published about her husband. She was willing to talk with historians about him and shared her information with those who asked.[6] Ursula was an avid record keeper who not only saved all her correspondence with her husband, but went through his papers, typed lists of the records and other notes, and finally gave the collection to the *Bundesarchiv*. After she died, her children became the caretakers of their father's memory.

In addition to the diaries and letters in Backe's personal collection, I also used the personal papers of Darré. Darré left an even larger personal collection than Backe, and he himself kept a diary. This diary, however, was edited by Hanns Deetjen after the war "for a small circle of Darré's closest friends." He used excerpts from the diaries and burned the original notebooks.[7] Its use for the historian is therefore questionable. His letters, however, are preserved and can be found in the city archives (*Stadtarchiv*) in Goslar as well as in the collection in the Institute for Contemporary History (*Institut für Zeitgeschichte*) in Munich. Here, we even find the many letters to Darré that his first and second wives wrote to him. Darré, in the limelight of political research as the long-term Minister of Food and Agriculture, was tried in Nuremberg during the Wilhelmstrasse Trial (November 1947 to April 1949). The protocols of the trial provide us with a lot of information about this man's politics. These sources have served as a foundation for my investigation of the relationship between Darré and his mentor-turned-rival Backe, and have been published elsewhere.[8]

The diaries and letters in the Backe files provided me with a very personal perspective, allowing me to shed light on the man behind the politics and see the connections and motivations of his actions. This final product of my efforts is, of course, not the biography that I had originally intended to write, since while planning my work, I realized that the format was too limiting. I instead chose to use the personal story as the basis of a wider historical study around which the chapters in this book are grouped. Herbert Backe is at the center of this story, a story with numerous perspectives all interconnected by the topics of food and agricultural politics.

CHAPTER OVERVIEW

This book is the first to comprehensively address the topic of food during the Third Reich. Food played a central political role for the Nazi regime and was vital in keeping up morale, in preparing Germany for war, in coming to terms with Germany's dependency on food imports, and finally as the foundation of a racial ideology that justified the murders of millions of Jews, prisoners of war (POWs), and Slavs. Early on, the Nazis recognized the elemental power of food as an instrument of persuasion for the masses and successfully used the topic as a propaganda tool to stir up support, to rally German people behind their *Führer* Adolf Hitler, and to instill fear and control throughout the country. While a great number of books have informed us about the workings of the Nazi State and its genocidal policies during World War II, the significance of food has remained largely unexplored. We know little about food culture during the Third Reich, how considerations and decisions touching on the production and acquisition of food affected the war, how the Nazis used it as a weapon in their murderous campaign against the Soviet Union, and to what extent food shortages expedited the Final Solution—the genocide of European Jews. We have heard about the misery of Soviet POWs and about the starvation of civilians in Leningrad, but the approximately four to seven million people killed as a consequence of Nazi food policy have received relatively little attention.

This book highlights the importance of food in Nazi ideology, its use as a justification for war, and as a tool for genocide. It examines the economics and the politics of food production, distribution, and consumption. Food rationing was prominent in most countries during World War II, but the availability of food varied widely from country to country and from one social group to another. Compared to World War I, Germany was better prepared and able to prevent widespread hunger among Germans at home. Ruthless exploitation of their allies and occupied countries ensured that most Germans had enough to eat throughout the war. The same was not true for their enemies. Drastic plans were made for the economic plunder of the Soviet Union, and the ultimate goal was to restructure the European continental market according to German needs. Slavs featured in this plan as slave laborers to German farmers, while large numbers of people were to be resettled or killed outright. In the wake of the invasion of the Soviet Union, hunger and starvation became a powerful weapon used against people considered to be racially inferior and unworthy consumers of precious food resources. Some three million German soldiers on the Eastern front were told to take whatever resources they needed from the countries they invaded, and to send anything above and beyond their immediate needs to their families in Germany.

During the Barbarossa campaign, millions of Soviet soldiers in German captivity and civilians in Soviet cities died of hunger and starvation.

This fate was not the unexpected consequence of a war that took longer than anticipated. It was the calculated strategy of a small group of economic planners and Nazi bureaucrats. The consequences of their decisions, made in closed meetings, can be compared to the outcome of the well-known *Wannsee* conference in January 1942 that sealed the fate of European Jewry. The mass murder in the occupied territories of the Soviet Union caused by Nazi food policy has not yet received the same attention, but this is about to change.

The central figure of this book is Herbert Backe, the second Reich Minister of Food and Agriculture. He was the Food Commissioner in the Four-Year Plan administration that prepared Germany for war and took over Richard Walther Darré's responsibilities as Reich Minister in 1942. His name has long escaped most history books and has only recently resurfaced in public. Backe was one of the authors of the *Hungerplan*, a plan that foresaw the starvation of tens of millions of Soviet citizens in cities and other regions. He was not the sole mastermind behind this plan, but the examination of his role and motivation offers great insight into Nazi ideology, food policies, and their murderous consequences.

The book is divided into six chapters. Chapter 1 examines the importance of food in Nazi ideology. Early on, propaganda about food was used to garner support for the Nazi Party and to increase its electoral success. Once in power, food continued to be central to the Nazis' portrayal of Hitler as the savior who would bring Germany out of the economic crisis and reestablish the country as a great power. The hunger and suffering of German civilians during World War I served as a warning example of the mistakes that had to be avoided at all costs. The Allied blockade and the threat of famine had, according to the Nazis, weakened support for the war, spread resistance, and had ultimately caused the collapse of the home front. Food, or the shortage thereof, was thus responsible for Germany's defeat in World War I and for the shameful Treaty of Versailles. The economic crisis and suffering of civilians had continued after the war. The Nazis would never forget this lesson.

The greatest importance of food lay in its role in preparing Germany to fight a war that would undo the injustice of Versailles. This war would provide *Lebensraum* or "living space" for German settlers, soil for German peasants to farm, and it would reorganize the European continental market under German control. The ambitious goal of achieving food autarky, or economic self-sufficiency, would link food policies to a racial war that would destroy millions of people.

Chapter 1 also examines the ideology of "blood and soil," an agrarian ideology that would remain one of the pillars of Nazi thought until the very end of the Third Reich. It portrayed peasants as the foundation of the German nation and elevated farming to one of the most honorable professions. It made peasants feel "secure" in the face of industrialization, foreign competition, and structural change that threatened their way of life. The Nazi regime went to great lengths to ensure the peasantry's compliance with the regime and to secure agricultural production. They staged elaborate ceremonies that celebrated the peasants' contributions and their cultural value to Germany. These efforts paid off. Most peasants continued to produce, and while they resented the close oversight and tight controls, their grumbling did not become a serious threat to the regime.

Chapter 2 looks at what Germans ate and how they adapted to the war economy. While the Nazis strove to make Germany independent of food imports, the limitations of domestic agriculture and food production put serious strains on the food economy. To avoid shortages and social revolt, Germany had to be prepared for a war and increase its food resources. The Four-Year Plan administration, founded in 1936 under the leadership of Hermann Göring, attempted to raise German agricultural production. To achieve this goal, the countryside and all people involved in food production, distribution, and consumption, had to be brought in line. A massive organization was formed, known as the Reich Food Estate (*Reichsnährstand*), which oversaw every aspect of agricultural production and secured continuous food resources.

In preparation for war, the Nazi officials designed a complex food rationing system that would stretch limited resources and maintain the public image of fair distribution. In 1936, they proclaimed the "battle for food" (*Ernährungsschlacht*) that was to increase production significantly. When these measures were not enough to satisfy hungry stomachs, Nazi propaganda set out to change eating habits. The Nazis promoted a new diet that made use of locally grown food, leftovers, and *Ersatz* ("substitute") foods. They praised Spartan eating habits and "one-pot meals" (*Eintöpfe*). "Eating right" became a patriotic exercise. The new food regimen greatly disadvantaged Jews and the many forced laborers in Germany who were employed in industry and agriculture to make up for the loss of male workers in those areas. Overall, the carefully designed food policies worked—most Germans on the home front had enough food to survive throughout the war. This would change only in the last year of hostilities. By that time, hunger had been exported on a grand scale to people in the occupied countries, to prisoners of war and Jews in ghettos and concentration camps all across Europe.

Chapter 3 focuses on Herbert Backe in the Reich Ministry of Food and Agriculture, the man who stood at the center of food politics. In a short span of time, Backe rose from failed academic to influential food minister and close confidant of Adolf Hitler, Hermann Göring, and Heinrich Himmler. He quickly outflanked his former boss and mentor, Reich Minister of Food and Agriculture, Richard Walther Darré. Darré felt increasingly outcast by the other Nazi leaders, even though his ideas continued to be employed and remained pillars of Nazi ideology until the final collapse of the regime. Backe was born in the Russian Empire to German immigrants and grew up in the Caucasus, a region at the border of Europe and Asia by the Black Sea. He spent his childhood immersed in Russian language and culture, but as a German, he was treated as an enemy during World War I and interned for years in a small mountain village. After this, he would turn against the people he grew up with and, as the "Russia expert" among Nazi leaders, would have the last say in determining their fate. Under Backe's leadership, more than two million Soviet POWs died of hunger and starvation in German camps. In addition to these casualties many civilians in the cities, also cut off from adequate food supplies, finally succumbed to hunger as well. If Backe's policies had been even more successful, tens of millions more would have perished. Only the failure of the Barbarossa campaign—the invasion of the Soviet Union in June 1941—and the impracticality of his "hunger plan" prevented this from happening on the enormous scale he had predicted. The number of people who died as a consequence of Nazi food policy surpasses the devastation of many other of the notorious famines in world history.

Chapter 4 looks in detail at Backe's so-called *Hungerplan* ("huger plan"). The focal point is the role that food played in the German invasion of the Soviet Union. Long before the actual attack began on June 22, 1941, Hitler had used ideological and economic reasons to justify the planned invasion of his "ally." The nonaggression pact of August 1939 had never been more than a tactical move on Hitler's part to prepare for the ultimate war in the East. Considerations of food supplies coupled with racial ideas made the war against Stalin's empire a high priority. SS task forces (*Einsatzgruppen*) followed the German Army to "cleanse" the territory of Jews, Communists, and partisans, and soldiers were charged with extracting agricultural surpluses from the conquered land to send back to Germany. After the quick defeat of the enemy, the Nazis planned to reorganize the territory in the East, remove native populations and settle German farmers on the land. The Greater German Reich would establish itself as the dominant power and master of continental Europe.

To ensure the efficient exploitation of food, economic preparations for Operation Barbarossa had begun much earlier. Herbert Backe knew of the planned invasion shortly after the military leadership received its orders in the winter of 1940–1941. He was charged to ensure provisions for the invading German Army and to design a plan to acquire the maximum of resources from the conquered soil. Backe agreed that all three million German soldiers should be fed from Russian soil alone. All food was to be taken at the expense of Soviet civilians. Backe warned his men of any "misdirected pity" for the Soviets, since they were "used to hunger" and were responsible for their own misery. Backe came up with a hunger plan (*Hungerplan*) that divided the Soviet Union into two zones, the "surplus" zone that consisted of the naturally rich areas of the Ukraine, southern Russia, the Caucasus region, and the "deficit" zone—the industrial and urban regions of Belarus, and northern and central Russia. The deficit zone was to be sealed off from all food supplies and people were left there to starve. Germans were to exploit the agricultural production in the Ukraine and the Caucasus for their own needs and any surplus would be sent home.

The chapter illustrates how food policy became genocidal policy during the campaign against the Soviet Union. The *Hungerplan* condemned hundreds of thousands of civilians in cities like Leningrad to death by starvation, and it also became a major weapon against the foremost enemy, the Soviet soldier. During the first year of the Barbarossa campaign, Germany took three million Soviets as prisoners. Two million of them died in German custody, most of them as a direct result of minimal food rations. The mass dying was intentional. It was the outcome of a racial policy that regarded Soviet people as inferior and dispensable.

While the mass murder of the Soviet POWs is no longer disputed, the implication of food politics for the pace and implementation of the Final Solution, the genocide of European Jews, is more controversial. More research has to be done to determine how food shortages and agricultural concerns radicalized the decision-making process and ultimately expedited the deportation of Jews to death camps. While hunger and disease had been among the main killers in the ghettoes and prison camps in Poland since the beginning of the war, German concerns about food supplies also influenced the timing of the transportation of hundreds of thousands of Jews still alive in Europe to the killing centers.

Nazi ideology brought changes to almost every aspect of German culture and society. The sciences were no exception. Rather than simply using the sciences to legitimize their policies with (pseudo-)scientific arguments, scientists and the regime collaborated closely on many levels and various research projects. Chapter 5 looks at how agricultural sciences fared under the Nazis, and how the sciences contributed to their goals and visions. Scientific research conducted at the prestigious Kaiser Wilhelm institutes that was deemed important for the war effort, for example, received increased funding. Other projects that would help achieve greater food autarky were also sponsored, and new opportunities opened up for scientists who received access to sensitive data or could experiment with human "guinea pigs" in concentration camps. The occupation of lands in the east brought new agricultural and geographic areas within close reach, regions whose natural and human resources could easily be exploited.

Two scientific studies serve as examples of how scientists collaborated with the Nazi regime. The food chemist Heinrich Kraut and his team examined the relationship between food intake and labor productivity among POWs. Joachim Caesar, who held a degree in agricultural sciences, grew plants in nurseries and laboratories near Auschwitz that exploited the free labor of internees from the concentration camp. To further their research and secure generous state funding, these scientists compromised their moral standards and thus contributed to the stability of the regime. Their findings made important contributions to Germany's war economy.

In the context of the science of food, chapter 5 also addresses the Nazis' relationship with nature and organic food. The question of "how green" the Nazis were has been raised repeatedly in recent historiography, and the answers have stirred up considerable debate.[9] While it is not relevant for the historical record if Hitler ate only vegetarian food or if he was a friend of animals, the debate over the Nazis' approach to nature and their stewardship of nature is highly illuminating and contributes to the understanding of the Nazi era. Hitler's vegetarianism, Himmler's sympathies for occult spirituality and Darré's fascination with alternative farming methods such as biodynamic or anthroposophic farming are thus interesting facets of the story. In the end, it seems unquestionable that the Nazis were a lot more "brown" than "green" even if their legislation of nature conservation was groundbreaking.[10]

The last chapter describes how hunger arrived in Germany during the last year of the war. The collapse on the military front was accompanied by a complete breakdown of the food regime. The loss of territory took away crucial resources of food, and the destruction of cities, agricultural land, and infrastructure inhibited the distribution of the little food that was available. The food crisis took on a critical dimension in the face of millions of refugees who poured into Germany, mainly Germans who fled the advancing Soviet army in formerly German or German-occupied territories. The victorious Allies faced a dramatic situation at the end of the war, and the increasingly frigid political climate of the Cold War inhibited any cooperation to deal with the crisis. Chapter 6 also analyzes the end of the main players in Nazi food politics, their trial in the Nuremberg war crime trials, and their remembrance in postwar Germany. The chapter concludes with an examination of how the postwar hunger years were replaced by a wave of gluttony (*Fresswelle*). The economic recovery in Western Germany in the early 1950s was so dramatic that the social transformation appeared simply "miraculous" to many contemporary observers. The decade also saw the coming together of European countries in an economic community that promised a new era of prosperity and plenty of food for Europeans.

There are no books published on food during the Third Reich. Studies of agricultural policies exist that include food policies, the rationing system, and the economic planning of the invasion of the Soviet Union; but the focus of these books is not on food itself.[11] Richard W. Darré, the Minister of Food and Agriculture, is well known and has received attention in literature,[12] but Herbert Backe's role has only recently been examined more closely.[13] Historians have written important studies on the connection between expansionist plans in the East and agricultural policies,[14] while most recently some authors have drawn attention to the famine among Soviet civilians caused by German Nazi aggression.[15] The fate and starvation of Soviet POWs were first highlighted in the 1970s but still need to be linked to the larger theme of food and agricultural policies.[16] The connection between the Nazis and the sciences has recently received greater attention, and important studies have been published examining individual scientists and research institutes during the Nazi era.[17] All of these findings can be related to the topic of food. Several works explore the relationship between "the green and the brown,"[18] while others describe peasant life during the Nazi regime or Nazi agricultural food policy.[19] My own research on Nazi agricultural politics started more than a decade ago, and some of the findings have been published in articles or book chapters.[20] Some of these works are only available in German, and none of them provide a comprehensive understanding of the topic of Nazi hunger politics in the Third Reich. This book intends to fill this gap.

A NOTE ON LANGUAGE

To tell the story of food in the Third Reich, any scholar would come across many German names and expressions that are difficult to translate. Even if a translation is available, the English words do not always capture the exact German meaning. The word *Bauer* or "peasant" can serve as one example of this dilemma. While *Bauer* in German is a common term for people who make a living in agriculture, its English translation peasant has a different and somewhat negative connotation. It brings to mind an ignorant tiller of the soil in premodern times, somebody of the past or somebody who has not adjusted to industrial production. In the United States, the term is slightly pejorative. There are—and never were—any peasants here, only farmers. Germany's small agricultural producers, however, have always—often proudly—called themselves *Bauern* long after industrialization changed agricultural production. During the Third Reich, the term was used purposefully and proudly. *Bauern* were celebrated in grandiose ceremonies and the word implied an honorable profession and honorable people. This positive self-identification as peasants continued after the Nazi era. The main agrarian interest organization in Germany calls itself the "German Peasant Organization" (*Deutscher Bauern Verein*) and uses this name even in the twenty-first century.

A term from the realm of food serves as another example for the difficulty of translation. As described in a later chapter, the "one-pot meal" or *Eintopf* became a favorite and symbolic dish consumed by many German families. It is a sort of stew that can be made with a great number of different ingredients. Root vegetables and potatoes are most often used, but meat can be added as well as other vegetables. The word, as its name so clearly expresses, refers to the ingredients all being cooked in a single pot. The Nazis vigorously promoted this dish and its many recipe varieties, since it could be made with lesser amounts of food or substitute foods and tasted good even with leftovers as ingredients. It was thus in line with the Nazis' idea of Spartan or austere cooking at a time when food resources were scarce and needed to be stretched as far as possible.

The translation of words and names forms a special challenge for anybody working with more than one language. The unique primary sources used in this study (most importantly, Ursula Backe's diaries) were of course all originally written in German. All translations of primary sources used in this book are the responsibility of the author, unless noted otherwise. My one impractical wish as an author is that I could write this book in both German and English, because I know there are people in Germany—my father is one example—who will not be able to read it because it is in English.

1

NO MORE TURNIPS

The Importance of Food in Nazi Ideology

Acquiring and sustaining sufficient food supplies was vital to the planning of the Third Reich. Not only was it necessary to satisfy the daily needs of the people in preparing for war, but also to decrease the country's dependence on food imports. Food served as the rationale for a war that would make land available to settle German farmers and provide Germany with plenty of natural resources. Food distribution was also instrumental for a racial ideology that justified the murder of millions of Jews, POWs, and Slavs. Last but not least, food became a powerful weapon in the destruction of Germany's foremost enemy, Stalin's Soviet Union. Food policy featured prominently in the planning for *Operation Barbarossa*—the German invasion of Russia in 1941—and ultimately turned into genocidal policy. This chapter scrutinizes the importance of food for Nazi ideology from the Nazis' earliest propaganda campaigns in the 1920s, to the celebration of "Blood and Soil" in the 1930s, and throughout the six years of war. The experience of World War I, when Germans at home had gone hungry and their support for the war faltered, was pivotal for the Nazis' ideology and their rise to power.

TURNIPS AND NOTHING ELSE: THE EXPERIENCE OF HUNGER DURING WORLD WAR I

The Nazis' concern with food had its origins in the widespread experiences of hunger and defeat among the population during World War I. Immediately after the German invasion of Belgium in August 1914, the British had responded to the violation of Belgium's neutrality with a sea blockade. All food imports as well as the delivery of raw materials destined for Germany transported via the North Sea were intercepted. The British Royal Navy patrolled the waters of the North Sea, sank German ships, and diverted neutral ones suspected of carrying food to Germany to British ports where they were checked. The Allies worked together to implement the blockade. A trade agreement prohibited neutral countries from bringing foods to Central Europe and trade restrictions were enforced in case of noncompliance. The consequences of the blockade for German civilians were immediate and severe. Germany had planned on a short war and had therefore not engaged in any serious emergency planning. Government officials had also expected Great Britain to stay out of the conflict and no preparations had been made for a scenario that involved being cut off from food imports. There were no reserves to count on and domestic production could not be augmented.[1] Shortages and hunger quickly became the reality of life for many civilians. It would be precisely this kind of hunger crisis that the Nazis vowed not to repeat twenty years later.

A variety of factors turned the blockade into a catastrophe for German consumers. Germany had depended heavily on the import of food long before the outbreak of war in 1914. With the accelerated industrialization in the last half of the nineteenth century, Germany had primarily focused on the creation of markets for its industrial goods. This in turn had left the country to rely more and more on the import of foods and raw materials. In response to pressure from agrarian interests groups, the German government had erected high tariffs for the import of agricultural goods in the 1880s, but this kind of agrarian protectionism stood in contrast with the interest in free trade for industrial products. In the 1890s, the protection continued in the form of tax reductions and export subsidies for agricultural producers. By the beginning of World War I, about onc-third of all Germany's foodstuffs came from outside the country.[2] Germany's dependency on other countries was especially high for proteins (27 percent) and fats (42 percent).[3] In addition to the dependence on food imports, domestic food production was severely impacted by the war itself. Fertilizer and ammunition were both produced from the chemical compound ammonium nitrate, but since the war had priority, major industries were redirected to produce ammunition and other military necessities. The dramatic shortage of chemical fertilizers gravely affected agricultural production, and the deterioration in infrastructure amplified the food crisis. The military draft of farm laborers left the countryside with fewer hands to work the fields.[4] Since draft animals were confiscated as well, there was not enough man- and horsepower to bring in the harvest and sufficiently farm the lands. By the end of the war a total of nine hundred thousand POWs worked as farm workers in Germany, but this was not enough to make up for the shortage.[5]

The effects of the sea blockade were felt immediately. Prices for food went up quickly. A fifty-pound sack of potatoes formerly available in Munich for three marks was sold for nine marks shortly after the announcement of war.[6] The price hikes simply left large parts of the population without the means to buy enough food. To ensure that consumers had something to eat, the government intervened in food production and distribution. It started with the regulation of prices for certain foods, and by the end of the war the production, distribution, and consumption of every food item was heavily controlled. The oversight even included the so-called *Ersatz* foods or substitute foods that were introduced to replace products no longer available on the regular market. Instead of coffee beans, for example, acorns and beans were roasted to create a drink that if nothing else resembled brewed coffee.

The government also tried to regulate the food market by establishing price ceilings to ensure the affordability of food. The first price ceilings were introduced for grain in October 1914, followed by set prices for potatoes in November. The prices, however, varied greatly from region to region. This had the effect that products were increasingly sold on the black market at substantially higher prices. Food was thus taken out of regular circulation and became even scarcer. The government saw no other way than to subject more and more food items to state control. Food rationing began in larger cities at the beginning of 1915. In Berlin, for example, citizens received weekly rations of bread only if they were in possession of a "bread card" (*Brotkarte*). War Boards (*Kriegsgesellschaf-*

ten) were established to oversee the rationing of flour, oats, butter, eggs, potatoes, and other products.

In addition to the tight oversight, the government also used propaganda to alleviate the situation. "Meatless days" or substitute foods were heavily promoted. All of the efforts, however, proved insufficient. As early as 1916, many civilians in the cities faced severe food shortages. The unequal distribution of existing resources further added to the crisis. Three years into the war, many could barely survive. The widespread malnutrition weakened the bodies' resistance to illnesses and caused high mortality and low fertility rates all across the country. In the end, hunger and starvation had become the daily reality for many Germans. More than seven hundred thousand people would die of hunger in Germany over the course of the war.[7]

The precarious food situation threatened the social peace and undermined the *Burgfrieden*—literally "castle peace truce"—that had united Germans at the beginning of the war.[8] Consumers were increasingly infuriated by rumors about food producers in the countryside who allegedly hoarded foodstuff and profiteered from the shortages by selling goods on the black market. Consumers vented their anger in loud protests against farmers and local administrations. The government knew no other way than to respond with even more severe control of food production. Peasants had to declare their stores of agricultural products and were not allowed to use wheat, rye, or bread to feed their animals. They were punished severely if they did not comply with the strict regulations.[9] The farming community strongly resented this close supervision.

But it was the cities that came to be the major centers of unrest. Here, food supplies and overall living conditions became more and more desperate. "War kitchens" were set up in the cities by relief organizations that provided a warm meal—usually soup—to needy families. Unaffordable food prices and widespread scarcity of food became the main source of discontent and led to the first food riots in Berlin in the autumn of 1915. Over the next years, the situation would get much worse for Berliners and other urbanites. The 1916 rations were meager, and the so-called *Ersatz* food became the only food available. Meat all but disappeared from the diet of lower-class families, and enraged consumers spent hours waiting in food queues in front of stores, often to find nothing left for them to buy for their hungry families. The potato became the main source of nutrition, and by early 1916 its consumption had more than doubled compared to prewar levels. When a wet fall in 1916 destroyed half of the potato harvest, the consequences for much of the populace were disastrous. People turned to the turnip which had a somewhat sour taste and was commonly used as food for animals. This root vegetable was to become the most versatile Ersatz food. It was used in soups, to make bread, as a meat substitute, and even in coffee. To make coffee, the turnip was to be cut up into small pieces, dried in the oven, and ground. Numerous cookbooks were published that suggested different ways to use the unpopular root to create meals. Germans who lived through this would always remember the "turnip winter" as an especially hard time. The recollections of Walter Koch from the Food Ministry in Saxony, are typical:

> Especially painful was seeing my children. I still see them, the 15-year-old Manfred and the 11-year-old Vera, coming home from school. Without a word they went straight to the pantry looking on the shelves for something to put into their empty stomachs. The saddest thing were the struggles with my wife, who gave her already small portions to the children and risked her health by doing so. We ate 5 or 6 centner (250–300 kg) of turnips in that horrible winter. Turnip soup in the morning, breaded and roasted turnip for lunch and turnip cake in the evening. And we were better off than hundreds of thousands of others, especially those in border regions.[10]

People mockingly dubbed the turnip the *Hindenburg-Knolle* (*Hindenburg "tuber"*), named after General Paul von Hindenburg, the popular chief of general staff and victor at the battle of Tannenberg in 1914.[11]

The turnip remained the staple of the German diet throughout the remaining two years of the war. The loss of the potato had triggered a chain reaction. Since meat and potatoes were in short supply, people turned to bread. The so-called *Kriegsbrot* ("war bread") was to be made with 20 percent potato flour. Since there were not enough potatoes to meet the demand, bread was made of rye and a range of substitutes that were hard to digest.[12] Even *Kriegsbier* (war beer) was made with substitutes. This much less enjoyable drink contained less than 4 percent alcohol. Coffee and tea entirely disappeared from the homes and if brewed at all, coffee consisted of a substitute mixture of carrots and turnips.[13]

Shortages in animal fodder was another area of concern. Germans were asked to collect and deliver acorns, beechnuts, dried fruit peels, and other items that could be used as fodder substitutes. The deficiency in fodder seriously affected the already tight supplies of milk, meat, and fats. In an act of desperation, the order was given to slaughter livestock on a grand scale to preserve turnips and potatoes, commonly used to feed pigs, for human consumption. The notorious "pig murder" (*Schweinemord*) was highly controversial—and disastrous in its consequences. In spring 1915, farmers were ordered to slaughter their pigs to reduce the need for fodder. By the last year of the war, the number of pigs had been reduced by 77 percent. The slaughter of all pigs, however, did little to improve the supply of potatoes. Pork simply disappeared from the public view and could only be bought on the black market. The directive remained just one of the many desperate actions of the government to alleviate the food crisis.[14]

The "pig murder" and the turnip winter affected everybody's mood and attitude toward the war. People lamented the unfairness of food distribution and suffered from the physical effects of malnutrition. Among the first victims were working-class children and the elderly. Overall, the death rate increased while the birth rate dropped dramatically. In 1918, child mortality was almost twice as high as it had been before the war.[15] Stories of how mothers sacrificed their health to feed children and husbands are well documented, and historical research has established that overall, girls suffered more than boys, women more than men.[16] If starvation wasn't the main cause of death, malnutrition did lower the body's resistance to diseases and infections and ultimately caused death. Even after the war, tuberculosis and the Spanish influenza took a heavy toll.[17]

The widespread misery made the topic of food omnipresent. Pamphlets drew attention to the connection between other resources (such as coal and bread) and food production, while advice books were published on how to make ends meet with reduced food supplies. Cookbooks encouraged housewives to make "delicious" meals with the Ersatz food, and posters urged the public to "be economical with bread." "War bread"—*Kriegsbrot*, referred to simply by the letter "K" in government propaganda—was praised as a good substitute made with rye and potato flour. But the popular discontent continued to spread. The anger targeted the government and civilian authorities. People were enraged by their belief that there would be enough to eat were it not for the failures of the food administration, an unfair distribution system, private hoarding—and the peasants. As a measure of appeasement, the government reacted with a propaganda campaign that defended its food policy, asking the population to "hold out" just a little longer.[18] Another tactic used in the campaign was to divert attention from domestic problems to the devious enemy, who was blamed for the suffering. In one of the posters, an Englishman was depicted with a vicious looking bulldog. Big letters at the top of the poster announced that "He is responsible!" (see figure 1.1). The text in smaller font read: "While Germans have to fight and bleed, have to go without, must save on coal and lightening, need ration cards and food coupons, and can't follow their peacetime work, the real enemy is England!" The poster then called Germans to "Remain united! Remain strong! That way you will secure Germany's victory!"

Germany was not the only country affected by the war shortages. France saw its rations drop during the war, but catastrophic shortages similar to the ones in Germany could be avoided. Great Britain introduced rations as well, but here the daily calories were much higher than the average German rations. In Great Britain, food distribution functioned reasonably well and the people did not perceive the system as unjust. The British government used the topic of food to stir up support and war enthusiasm, while in Germany food was clearly the topic that divided and antagonized Germans. In Britain, housewives were encouraged to use the limited available resources creatively. Wartime cookbooks suggested ways to compensate for scarce ingredients (especially meat and sugar) and encouraged the use of unfamiliar ingredients to make up for the missing calories. The tone of these cooking instructions was cheerful and emphasized the common experience. Nellie De Lissa, a cooking instructor for the Middlesexes County Council, wrote a book published in 1915 that according to her own words was

> intended as an aid to housewives to whom existence under the new conditions is a problem, and also to their more fortunate sisters who have the means and the will, and perhaps not the practical knowledge, as to how they may economize and thus indirectly make things easier for others less generously provided with the needful.[19]

She added that the book "is simply a practical attempt to help my sisters in the hard winter months which we must all face cheerfully and to assure to them the 'contented mind' which a well-lined stomach never fails to give."[20] De Lissa described the new conditions in British households and made suggestions on how to provide good meals with less food, how to

Figure 1.1. "He Is Responsible." Source: Bundesarchiv Plak 001-003-001.

avoid waste, and how to maintain a "pleasing variety" of meals with substitute foods.[21] "Nourishing soups" were considered to be an especially good meal, since they were satisfying and could be made with a variety of ingredients, even if meat was scarce:

> These are perfect foods in themselves and do quite completely take the place of meat, with less waste in the process of assimilation and with the additional advantage of giving warmth to the blood, and having a tonic effect on the stomach; and last, but not least, they are extremely cheap and easy to procure and to make into attractive food form.[22]

In all wartime countries, civilians bore the main brunt of the shortages. Soldiers across the board received much higher rations than their compatriots. Even in Germany, where the food distribution system had completely collapsed, soldiers received sufficient food to eat. A German soldier's daily ration was 3,200 calories at the beginning of war, and remained relatively high for most of the war. New methods were successfully used to feed front soldiers at the front. Food processing enterprises such as bakeries and slaughterhouses were set up in occupied areas and field kitchens cooked meals for them. The preferential treatment given to the military resulted in the fact that the army consumed 30 percent of total bread grains and 60 percent of all cattle and pork in 1918. Food provisioning of the German Army was sufficient "because civilians starved to ensure that the soldiers ate."[23]

While the Allied Blockade had no direct influence on the German offensive, the government considered its effect on the civilian morale serious enough to threaten the outcome of the war. In a desperate attempt to break the blockade and allow food imports, Germany declared unrestricted submarine warfare in March 1917. This strategy failed and brought hitherto neutral allies into the war. The United States declared war on Germany a few weeks later. The sinking of the ocean liner Lusitania with more than one hundred Americans onboard two years earlier had caused a storm of outrage in the United States and would eventually influence the decision to enter the war. Throughout the rest of the war, Germany could not lift the burden of the blockade and remained dependent on its own scarce domestic resources. The food situation thus remained desperate until the end of the war.

A VOTE FOR BREAD AND WORK? FOOD IN NAZI PROPAGANDA

Food shortages and hunger remained a daily reality for many Germans even after the war. The Allies continued their blockade beyond the German surrender on November 11, 1918. It was only lifted after the German government had agreed to the Allied demands and signed the Treaty of Versailles in June 1919. The Allies believed that the Hunger Blockade had deeply affected the civilian morale, and some worried that the long-term effects on the health of many Germans were detrimental to a quick recovery. It is impossible, however, to estimate to what degree the hunger blockade contributed to illness and mortality after the war. In any case, bodies weakened by extended periods of malnutrition certainly were less resistant to diseases such as Spanish influenza and succumbed quickly.

Even after the blockade was lifted, food production and distribution continued to be impacted. The widespread destruction caused by the war slowed down the economic recovery for years. In 1920, the German agricultural output was only half of the prewar level. The situation did not improve until the end of inflation in 1923, and only in 1928 would domestic food production reach prewar levels.[24] The traumatic experience of food shortages and hunger riots would play a pivotal role in the Nazis' myth building. To the Nazis, the food crisis had played into the hands of Socialists and Communists and had led to Germany's capitulation. Food riots had turned into general dissatisfaction with the national government and had caused revolutionary unrest. In the end, Germany lost the war not because of the defeat of the German Army but because of the betrayal of German civilians on the home front who had withdrawn their support for the monarchic government and pronounced a republic. This legend of the "stab in the back" (*Dolchstosslegende*) had thus germinated in the dire food situation: because of the food crisis, Germans withdrew their support for the war and forced the government to negotiate for peace.

For years after the war, food continued to be crucial for domestic stability and social peace. All political parties used the topic to garner support for their platforms and to win votes in parliamentary elections, but none of them exploited it to the same extent as the National Socialist German Workers Party (*Nationalsozialistische Deutsche Arbeiter Partei*, NSDAP or Nazi Party). The Nazis used the topic of food to depict its political enemies in the worst colors. "Bread, land, and peace" had been the battle cry of the Bolshevik Revolution. After the Bolshevik victory, the Soviets had plunged into a civil war and widespread famine had decimated the Russian population. The Nazis and other right-wing groups didn't miss an opportunity to emphasize that Germany would go down the same disastrous road if the political left had its way. Early propaganda posters showed the allegedly fateful connection between communism and hunger, and this would still set the tenor of the electoral campaign in 1932. The message in two posters from 1932 suggested that a regime led by Communists and Socialists would lead to "misery and hunger" (*Elend und Hunger*) while a vote for the NSDAP was depicted as a decision for "employment and bread" (*Arbeit und Brot*) (see figure 1.2), or "against hunger and desperation" (*Hunger und Verzweiflung*) (see figure 1.3).

The worldwide economic crisis after 1929 was the turning point for the Nazis' electoral success. In the elections following the crash of the New York stock exchange, the Nazi Party would turn from a small splinter party into the strongest party in the German parliament. Unemployment, economic crisis, and the memory of hunger and desperation drove many people to look for a leader who promised to bring Germany out of the crisis.[25] Nazi propaganda responded to this sentiment and depicted the Nazis as the ones who knew how to rebuild Germany. The building blocks needed for economic recovery were employment (*Arbeit*), freedom (*Freiheit*), and most importantly, bread (*Brot*)—a message that was displayed in a poster from April 1932 under the title "We Rebuild!" (*Wir bauen auf!*) (see figure 1.4).

The Nazis' electoral strategy worked. In the Reichstag election in July 1932, the Nazi Party became the largest party in the parliament, winning 37 percent of the vote. On January 30, 1933, after much intrigue and negotiation, President Paul Von Hindenburg appointed Hitler as the chancellor of Germany. Even after that, food continued to be central to the Nazis' self-portrayal. Hitler appeared as the savior who would bring Germany out of the economic crisis and reestablish the country as a great power. After eight months in power, the Nazis boasted during the October Reichstag election that Hitler had brought "work, freedom, and bread" to millions of German people.

ONE VOLK—ONE MEAL

The Nazis would never forget how important sufficient food was for the support of the regime and, after 1939, for the war. Hitler vowed that Germans would never again experience hunger.[26] Once the war started, a poster (see figure 1.5), showed children playing with strollers and dolls

Figure 1.2. "Misery and Hunger." Source: Bundesarchiv Plak 002-042-107.

and suggested "That's what we're fighting for—for our children's bread!!" (*Dafür kämpfen wir—für das Brot unserer Kinder!!*).

Figure 1.3. "Against Hunger and Desperation!" Source: Bundesarchiv Plak 002-016-050.

Domestic agricultural production had to increase if Germany wanted to become less dependent on food imports and achieve "nutritional free-

Figure 1.4. "We Rebuild!" Source: Bundesarchiv Plak 002-040-007.

dom." This was no easy task. Farmers had little means to invest in their farms and modernize agricultural production. The "flight from the land" continued, and once the war started, farm laborers were drafted into the

Figure 1.5. "For Our Children's Bread!" Souce: Bundesarchiv Plak 003-009-162.

army. The war profoundly changed the economic priorities, and producing "canons" became more important than "butter." Industries were redirected to produce ammunition and weaponry, as the support of the war effort became the main concern.[27] In recognition of these new realities, Nazi propaganda changed its tune. The new focus was on adjusting German food habits to alleviate the pressure on certain foods. Meat can serve as a prime example. To reduce the amount of meat and fodder that had to be imported, the advantages of grain and cereals were praised. Germans were encouraged to make simple and inexpensive meals and to use leftovers (*Resteverwertung*) creatively. The housewives' thriftiness with their ability to cook economically (*Sparsamkeit*) was considered a sacrifice worth making for the German nation. Housewives were to buy only German products, consumers were to eat rye bread instead of wheat bread, and the potato again was to become the main nutrient and most versatile ingredient in a German meal plan. The overarching motto was to "cook well with what we have." Brochures, cookbooks, and magazines offered plenty of advice and suggested tasty and easy recipes for economical cooking.

One of the most successful campaigns to change German eating habits was the promotion of the *Eintopfsonntag*, or "one-pot meals" to be eaten on Sunday.[28] The Winter Relief Agency (*Winterhilfswerk*) organized charity drives starting in October 1933 for which Germans were asked to prepare and eat a meal that was made with vegetables and inexpensive cuts of meat all cooked together in one dish. Soups or stews that were cooked in one pot were nothing new in German culinary history, but the term *Eintopf* was not coined until the early 1930s.[29] The Nazis used the term propagandistically to promote new eating habits. The *Eintopf* was to be eaten instead of the traditional and more expensive Sunday roast. The money saved by preparing the cheaper meal was to be donated to the *Winterhilfswerk*. Volunteers working for the charity went from door to door to collect the money—and to check if families had followed the directive. Restaurants, canteens, and other public kitchens were required to offer an *Eintopf* on Sundays as well. Many housewives responded favorably to the campaign. *Eintopfsonntage* were observed more and more often, magazines published recipes, and regions developed their own special variety. Ever so good at promoting a favorable picture of the Führer, Hitler was shown sharing such a meal together with others.[30] The *Eintopf* thus came to symbolize a lot more than just an inexpensive meal. The dish was prepared with German ingredients and lots of tasty leftovers and thus was the perfect recipe for the economical housewife. It tasted best in the company of family and friends and could easily feed a larger group of people. In addition to the economic advantages, the *Eintopf* took on a racial meaning. The *Ein-Topf* ("one pot") stood for a "mini-version of a Germanic *Ein-Volk*" (one people).[31] The dish thus symbolized the racial and organic community of Germans. Since everybody ate the same dish, class lines became less distinct. The *Eintopf* undermined bourgeois eating culture with its emphasis on fine table manners and social prestige.[32] A poster from 1936 promoting the *Eintopfsonntag* showed five happy children and a man helping themselves from one large pot. Several dates appear on the poster, indicating one Sunday of every month when the dish was to be eaten (see figure 1.6). The nourishing and healthy repast would bring Germans together, strengthen German bodies, and support the national economy all at the same time. Eating the *Eintopf* on Sunday became a quasi-religious ritual, and the Nazis emphasized the sacrificial nature of the occasion. A brochure of the *Winterhilfswerk* describes the meal in 1934 in the following way:

> Just as it has long been a custom on every Friday, in memory of the crucifixion of Christ, to fast or at least to only eat fish, so too has the casserole dish in the shortest of time become a popular German custom . . . the monthly casserole-eating brings us together to form a community that knows no hierarchy of class or birth . . . the casserole is the fasting-meal [*Fastmahl*] of the German nation. Just as faithful Christians unite in the holy sacrament of the last supper in service of their lord and master, so too does National Socialist Germany celebrate this sacrificial meal [*Opfermahl*] as a solemn vow to the unshakeable people's community.[33]

Recipes for an *Eintopf* varied greatly across Germany and could be made in multiple ways. A very common recipe was the *Erbseneintopf* or split pea soup made with dried peas, bacon cubes (*Speck*), and potatoes. It could be served with sausages (*Wiener* or *Knackwurst*). Even if the overall economic benefits of the *Eintopfsonntag* and other drives to promote simple and inexpensive eating habits (*Resteverwertung*) were moderate, it did have an effect on German consumption habits and morale. It prepared Germans for the scarcity of the war years, the tight rationing and increased use of *Ersatz* foods that would become the dire reality for years to come. Germans did not experience the kind of hunger that they had during World War I twenty years earlier—at least not for the first years of the war—but they had to make adjustments. The earlier campaigns prepared the way, and this time most Germans adjusted without too many complaints. The *Eintopf* itself would remain a staple of German cuisine until today. The fact that the Nazis basically invented the tradition is little known among contemporary Germans.[34]

Other propaganda campaigns followed along the same lines. Housewives were encouraged to make do with less and were advised on how to use leftovers. Whole wheat bread (*Vollkonrbrot*) was promoted as a substitute for white bread, since white flour had become a luxury item and had to be imported. The campaigns depicted rye bread as a healthier alternative, and the "sacrifice" to give up certain foods became a "patriotic duty." In a propaganda poster from 1939, healthy- and happy-looking children were shown crowding around their mother to get a slice of the rye bread she was cutting (see figure 1.7).

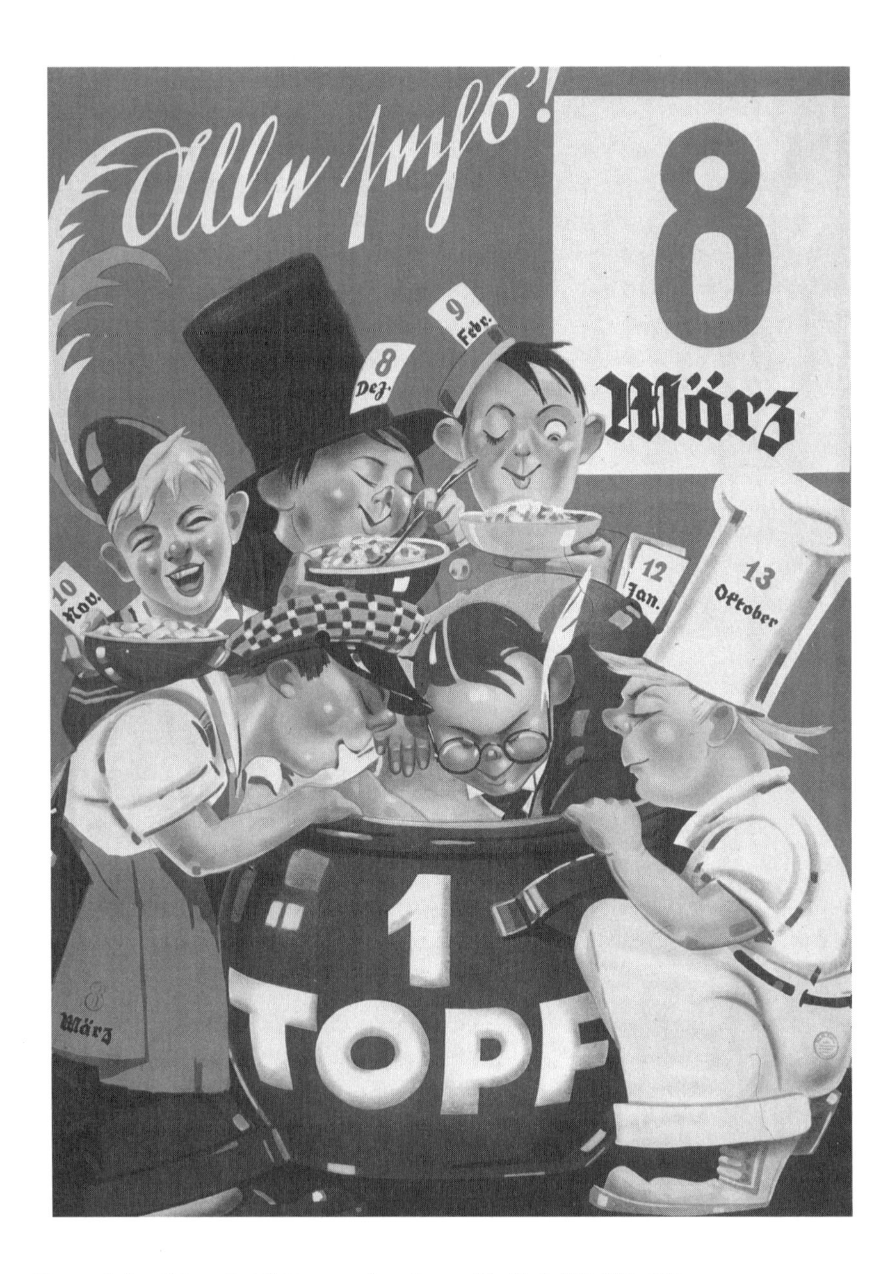

Figure 1.6. "One Pot." Source: Bundesarchiv Plak 003-016-031.

BLOOD AND SOIL IN THE 1930S

No matter how much Germans changed their eating habits, nutritional freedom had to start with the peasants. The new understanding of food and its relation to an "organic community" elevated the producers of food—the peasants—to a place of special importance for the future of the German people:

> No Volk can endure as long as it does not recognize than (sic) only one thing is eternal: blood and soil . . . he who produces food is thus as earthshaking [*weltbewegend*] as hunger itself; even those people who have the willpower to move mountains must eat in order to compose and to dream.[35]

Nazi Party strategists clearly understood the importance of winning over the peasants and keeping them happy throughout the Third Reich. The Nazi Party had originated in the early 1920s as an urban movement and had initially paid little attention to agricultural questions. This changed significantly in the last years of the Weimar Republic. In 1930, the Nazis had hired the agricultural expert Richard Walther Darré to organize the electoral takeover of the countryside. Darré fulfilled this task successfully. He first added agricultural goals to the Nazi platform, built up a political apparatus that reached every village, and brought rural interest groups solidly in line. By means of powerful propaganda, consistent pampering, and blunt coercion of those opposed to the Nazi platform, the countryside became the political backbone of Nazi support.[36]

Throughout the 1930s, the Nazis paid special attention to the countryside and rural populations. Darré developed a rural ideology that would become one of the most effective and persistent parts of Nazi ideology.[37] The ideology of "blood and soil" idealized the peasant as the healthy racial foundation of the German people. The praise of the peasant manifested itself in a variety of forms and was a staple of Nazi rhetoric until the collapse of the regime. Elaborate harvest celebrations were held, national "peasant days" instituted and the special value of the peasant popularized in pamphlets and Nazi publications. Darré became the "Reich Peasant Leader" and stood at the forefront of all peasant organizations. The praise of the peasants and their labor as the foundation of the German people and their state struck a chord with large parts of the rural population, which returned the recognition with unwavering political support.

Figure 1.7. "Eat Whole Wheat Bread." Source: Deutsches Historisches Museum, Berlin / I. Desnica.

The ideology of blood and soil celebrated peasants as the source of German economic and cultural vitality. Germans could look back at a long history of peasants who had settled down and formed villages. This, according to the ideology, had shaped the people, their morale, and character. Rural Germans rejected cities and urbanism and despised other nomadic people, especially the "desert-dwelling" Jews who lacked this presumed geocultural linkage of race and place.[38] Germany's survival and cultural dominance was allegedly built on this special connection between the German people (blood) and the land (soil). The accelerated industrialization and urbanization had threatened peasant farming in the late nineteenth century, and with it the very foundation of the German people. It thus became a priority for the Nazis to defend and preserve medium-sized peasant farms to restore Germany's "racial integrity."[39]

Long before the Nazis, however, others had explicitly made the connection between the words "blood and soil." In the nineteenth century, agrarian romanticists had stressed the "organic unity" of people and the soil and described peasants as the healthy "backbone" of society.[40] Ernst Moritz Arndt, an author and founder of the movement for German unification in the early 1800s, had called for the state to protect peasants as the foundation of the German people, and sociologist Wilhelm Heinrich Riehl had stressed the political value of peasants as a conservative bloc in society.[41]

With the emergence of "racial science" in the late nineteenth century, the idea of blood and soil took on a new connotation. Darré wanted blood to be understood as "race."[42] Peasants did not simply supply cities with "fresh blood" (people), but they were no less than the "life source of the Nordic race."[43] Darré spent time and energy on his idea to create a new ruling class that was rooted in the agrarian population.[44] His training as a specialist in genetic livestock selection allowed him to apply findings from animal breeding to human beings.[45] Just as in the animal world, the committed Social Darwinists believed in a system of racial selection that would create a new rural nobility to reach the "breeding goal of the German people."[46] Among the measures suggested by Darré were marriage restrictions for Jews and "less valuable" non-Jews, strict state control of all marriages and fertility, and the sterilization of those members of the community who were considered to be a threat to the "racial purity" of the German people. The Nazis used all of these measures in the subsequent years, even though the idea of a new rural political elite was never fully adopted.

In addition to the racial component, Darré added another important connotation to the idea of blood and soil. Nineteenth-century romanticists had thought of the soil as a source of character for the German people. Darré expanded the idea and used it to justify Germany's right to acquire land in the East and to settle ethnic Germans there. Germany was too small to produce enough food to become self-sufficient, and new territories were needed (*Lebensraum*).[47] People in the eastern lands were considered to be less capable of tilling the soil and settling down and could thus be dispersed. From the beginning, the Nazis agreed that this territory had to be taken by force. Hitler had written in 1925 in *Mein Kampf* (My Struggle) that "if one wants space and soil in Europe [Grund und Boden], this can really only be achieved at the cost of Russia" and use of the "German sword" as the means to win "soil for the German plow and daily bread for the nation."[48] Ukrainian fields were the "breadbasket" that Germany wanted to control—and believed it had every right to do so. For Germans to eat, others had to starve. The Nazis' hunger politics in the occupied eastern lands after the outbreak of the war found its justification in this agrarian ideology.[49]

With the preparation for war and the beginning of military conflict, peasants increasingly carried the burden to produce even more food under aggravating circumstances—low prices, forced deliveries, fewer farm hands, and the lack of investment. The appeal to their moral obligation and national responsibility thus became more important than ever. Many propagandistic publications and ceremonies publicly celebrated peasants as the producers of food who were vital and indispensable to the German people. In a radio speech in February 1940, Hitler's deputy Hermann Göring addressed the peasants directly and emphatically reminded them of their importance: "On your shoulders, peasants and farmers, peasant women and farm laborers, rests a double responsibility. Use all your energy. Show what you can do. The road ahead is endlessly hard and difficult."[50]

In return for their hard work and sacrifices, peasants were promised a new era after the war. Darré envisioned a Germany that would become a *Bauernreich* (peasants' empire) in which the agricultural sector would see large investments and modernization. Increased "living space" (*Lebensraum*) was crucial for the implementation of this vision, and peasants would be the ones settling and working the new lands. In addition to providing bread, peasants would thus play an important role in the future greater German Reich.

CELEBRATING THE PEASANTS: THE REICH HARVEST FESTIVAL ON THE BÜCKEBERG

It is impossible to measure how much peasants bought into Darré's abstruse ideas. Few of them would have read Darré's books or cared much about his "breeding goals." They did, however, welcome the importance attributed to them as the *Landvolk* ("peasantry") and *Nährstand* ("nurturing class") of the German nation. Peasants flocked to the carefully staged national celebrations of their harvest and responded to the display of everything that glorified the peasantry. The most impressive of these celebrations was the annual harvest festival on the Bückeberg, a hill or small mountain near the city of Hameln. Originally a holiday celebrated by Christian churches to thank God for a good harvest, Darré described it as the day when "the Germanic unity of peasant, soil, and creator are recognized as the most holy symbol of the connection between the Germanic people and the soil."[51] According to official figures, five hundred thousand people attended the first harvest festival in 1933. In 1937, the last time the annual harvest celebration was held, an estimated 1.3 million people attended the event.[52] Even if the Nazis exaggerated the number of attendees, there is no question about the great appeal of the spectacle.[53] The annual celebrations were more popular than the bombastic Nazi Party rallies held in Nuremberg. The appeal of the harvest celebration is an indicator of Darré's initial political clout and of agriculture's significance for the Nazi regime.

While the harvest festivals celebrated the peasants and their labor, they first provided a platform for the *Führer* to address the masses. It was also an opportunity to showcase Germany's military might. Every detail of these massive events was planned and staged like a military procession. The harvest symbols that were used in abundance served mostly as props for a message to be sent to the nation.

The attention to details started with the selection of the location. The Bückeberg ridge near the city of Hameln in Lower Saxony was chosen because of the far-reaching support for the Nazis in this northern German region. Lower Saxony had a strong agricultural base, and the nearby city of Hameln and its surroundings provided an infrastructure that could handle a spectacle of such scale. Lower Saxony also had great propagandistic value. The Nazis described it as a place that had seen extensive battles of the Germanic tribes which long ago had colonized and worked the land. The Weser River was called the "most German of all rivers,"[54] a river that "mirrored German greatness." The villages and proud peasant farms represented the "freedom fighter(s) embedded in the German soul."[55]

To create an appropriate meeting place for the festivities, Joseph Goebbels, Hitler's propaganda minister, hired one of his best men, the architect Albert Speer. The original design was kept simple to emphasize the peasant character of the event. It consisted of two stages connected by a long path and a large circular place surrounded by thousands of flagpoles. The stages and poles were made of wood. After the success of the first annual harvest celebration on the Bückeberg in 1933, Goebbels decided to turn the location into a Germanic cult place (*Reichsthingstätte*). Speer was again charged with the design. This time, a monument was to be built that would last for "eternity." Construction began immediately and lasted until 1937. Massive changes were made to the landscape, extensive roads were built to bring thousands of people to the festival, and train stations were redesigned. A new *Führerbahnhof* (the Führer's private train station) was built just for Hitler's arrival. To house the hundreds of thousands of visitors expected to arrive each year, camps were erected, and a pedestrian bridge was built. In typical Nazi attention to detail and staging, everything was planned out in minute detail, including the decoration of villages that lay en route to the Bückeberg and villages that would be visited by thousands of people on their way to the festival.[56]

The *Erntedankfest* was held for five consecutive years, with small changes to the carefully planned two-hour program. The 1937 festival was one of the biggest events ever held by the Nazis. More than one million people attended, according to official figures. Thousands of people arrived days before the actual beginning of the program. The visitors were housed in temporary barracks and nearby villages and enjoyed folkloristic entertainment throughout the weekend. Saturday's program included a military show and a dinner hosted by Goebbels for 150 selected peasant leaders. On Sunday morning the masses descended onto the *Festplatz* (festival grounds), marching toward it from all directions (see figure

1.9). Huge choirs with up to twenty thousand singers sang nationalistic songs throughout the morning, and the media was omnipresent with the task of distributing the images of the celebrated peasants throughout the Reich. The highlight of the celebration was the anxiously expected arrival of the *Führer* at 12 p.m. To get to the main stage located at the top of a hill, Hitler had to walk on the *Führerweg*, or the "path through the people," greeting them along the way (see figure 1.8).[57] The six hundred meters took him forty-five minutes, since many approached him for a handshake or a smile. Once on stage, Hitler received the "harvest crown" handed to him by a peasant woman, curiously the only active role performed by a woman throughout the program. Among the attendees, more than 60 percent were women.[58] After Goebbels had greeted the masses, a thirty-minute military demonstration was held. The event culminated in speeches given by Darré and Hitler. The whole program lasted two hours.

The Harvest Festival celebrated the peasant and peasant productivity, but the military overtones were hard to miss. The *Erzeugungsschlacht* ("battle of production") was to produce "bread from our own soil"—*Brot aus eigener Scholle*—and advance the goal of food autarky. The grandiose military demonstrations included "surprise" demonstrations with airplanes and panzers, and more than ten thousand men. Bridges were built across the Weser River and an "attack" on the "Bückedorf" was staged in minute detail.[59] Goebbels passionately summarized the highlights of the 1936 festival in his diary:

> An impressive procession to the top of the hill. The peasants nearly embrace him [Hitler]. He is our God. On the top of the hill, first the harvest wreaths. Then the great military demonstrations. Especially the air force. A unique spectacle! Huge attacks led by tanks. It is beautiful. The village of Meckerer is burning. Then we hear the firing.[60]

The prospect of war brought an end to the Harvest Festival. In 1938, with preparations for the celebration almost completed, the festivities were called off at short notice. The Czech crisis necessitated the redeployment of trains and military equipment that were needed for soldiers at the Czech border rather than for transporting peasants from across Germany to the Bückeberg in the north. The following year, the outbreak of war dramatically changed the priorities. While peasants and the fruits of their labor were still highly praised and indispensable for Germany to win the

Figure 1.8. Hitler greeting the masses on the Bückeberg. Source: Bundesarchiv Bild 146-1992-128-17A.

war, the economic necessities made such elaborate and expensive celebrations seem highly untimely.

***

Figure 1.9. Peasants in traditional costume or *Tracht*. Source: Bundesarchiv Bild 146-1992-128-00A.

The greatest importance of food in Nazi ideology lay in its role in preparing and sustaining Germany to fight a war that would undo the injustice of Versailles. This war would provide *Lebensraum* or "living space" for German settlers, and soil for German peasants to farm, and it would reorganize the European continental market under German control. The ambitious goal of achieving food autarky, or economic self-sufficiency, linked food policies to a racial ideology that would seal the fate of millions of people. Food, in the end, was the "economic incentive for murder on a scale larger even than the Holocaust."[61] It was the main ingredient of Nazi ideology and would inform the actions of the Nazis throughout the twelve years of their rule. The connection between food and war is more closely examined in the following chapter.

2

EATING AT HOME

Food Rationing and the Nazi Diet

During World War II, Germany exported hunger to millions of people outside the Reich. At the same time, most Germans at home had enough to eat, at least until the last winter of the war. Despite Germany's reliance on food imports that had made the country so vulnerable during the previous war, and despite the loss of male agricultural workers who were drafted into the military, the Nazi regime kept agricultural production going and maintained adequate food supplies. Nazi food policy, a tight food-rationing system, and the massive employment of foreign forced laborers in industry and agriculture ensured that Germans had something to eat. More importantly, the ruthless exploitation of conquered territories as well as supplies from its own apprehensive allies prevented food shortages similar to the ones experienced during World War I. This was true especially compared to other European countries where people suffered greatly under German domination. Citizens of Poland and the Soviet Union were cut off from food supplies in a deliberate starvation policy while millions of Soviet soldiers succumbed to hunger in German captivity and Jews in ghettos and concentration camp died from lack of food. At the same time, most German civilians had access to reliable food rations and were able to adjust to the circumstances and live with the shortages. They ate more potatoes and less meat than they had before and they made do with what was available. While hunger also existed within Germany, it was associated with moral and racial hierarchies. This chapter looks at what Germans ate during the Nazi years and how they adapted to the war economy.

CHANGES IN GERMAN FOOD CULTURE BEFORE 1933

When traveling in Germany today one will quickly notice great regional varieties of the cuisine. Each locality has its own specialties, and recipes vary from village to village. Germany's history of a mosaic of small and independent kingdoms, fiefdoms, and free cities prompted the development of these regional styles. During the latter half of the nineteenth century, industrialization and urbanization changed German eating habits and methods of food production, but the traditional differences continued.

German food habits have come a long way since the Roman period, when the Roman historian Tacitus (55–110 CE) depicted the Germanic "wild" tribes as surviving on fruits, game meat, and curdled milk.[1] Staples of the German diet such as pork and fish have been around for more than one thousand years and the production of wine has an equally long history. Germans' most popular drink, beer, was commercially produced and traded already in the second century CE. During the Middle Ages, oats, millet, and rye were added to the commonly used grains, wheat and barley. Throughout this era and during the early modern period, most Germans lived in small rural settlements and survived on what they produced themselves or what was left after their feudal shares were paid.

Urbanization brought changes in eating habits, since people who live in cities rather than on a farm have to buy most of the food they consume. The great majority of the population, however, continued to live from subsistence farming. Normally, they ate two warm meals a day (soups) supplemented with water and beer. A typical breakfast consisted of gruel, until bread made from rye gained in importance, especially in the northern parts of Germany.

During the late eighteenth century, Germany increased its imports of food from overseas. New foods such as coffee, potatoes, and drinks such as schnapps entered the German diet. At first, the potato was considered a food for the poor or was mostly used to feed animals. When people recognized the advantages of this versatile tuber, including the discovery that it could be used to make schnapps, the potato became one of the most important ingredients of ordinary people's meals. Other changes came along with the development of new food industries and food preservation methods in the nineteenth century. Gradually, the home production of pasta, *quark* (a white cheese similar to cottage cheese), other cheeses, jam, dried fruit, and pickled vegetables became less important while the methods of refrigeration and canning allowed for better storage and a longer life for food products.[2]

Agricultural modernization, the increasing use of chemical fertilizer, and mechanization allowed for a growth in production to feed the larger and more urban population. The greatest shift in food habits, however, occurred around the turn of the twentieth century with the growth of global markets. Increased wheat production in North America, Argentina, and Australia led to a fall in global grain prices. Britain was the first European power to outsource the growing of its food to colonies, and while Germany lagged behind in the race for an empire, its economy was rapidly expanding and more and more food was brought in from overseas. By the time the war broke out in 1914, Germany imported 20 percent of its food.[3] This dependence on imports was especially high for fats such as butter and margarine. Germany also imported great quantities of its dairy products, eggs, cattle fodder, and fertilizer.[4]

As chapter 1 illustrated, the dependence on imported foodstuffs, coupled with a lack of economic planning for a prolonged war, had made Germany vulnerable during World War I. A serious food crisis had led to widespread hunger and starvation and agricultural production continued to be impacted even after the end of the war. When the great inflation in 1923 erased any modest savings of the middle class, poverty affected large parts of the population. The slow recovery during the mid-1920s was halted by the worldwide economic crisis at the end of the 1920s, when the farming sector was hit especially hard in the economic downturn. Thousands of farms went bankrupt, and peasants all across Germany turned to radical parties in the desperate hope for change.[5] But hunger and desperation took hold also in the cities, where millions of unemployed people stood in line at soup kitchens. Not surprisingly, in this environment, the Nazis' promise to bring bread and work to Germany resonated well with people all across the country. By 1932, the Nazi Party had become the largest party in the German parliament.[6] On January 30, 1933, Hitler was appointed chancellor of Germany and the Third Reich had begun.

NUTRITIONAL FREEDOM AND THE NAZI DIET, 1933–1938

During the first six years of their rule, the Nazis did not miss a chance to depict themselves as the ones who had brought Germany out of its economic misery and who had delivered bread and employment for all.

In reality, the years of Nazi rule had done little to solve the problem of food shortages.[7] While the overall economic growth rate was high and unemployment had virtually disappeared—from six million or 34 percent unemployed in the winter of 1932–1933 to full employment in 1936—food production and consumption did not experience the same upward trend.[8] Domestic agricultural production did not increase and rising food needs caused by the expanding industrial sector put further pressure on food supplies.

In fact, by the mid-1930s, the general population had even less access to food supplies because of tighter food production and strict distribution and market controls. The prioritization of the armaments industry as well as the Nazi policy of achieving food autarky impacted food resources tremendously. The enforced limitations on imports reduced, for example, the number of cattle, with the effect that less beef was available in the stores for purchase. Some food items completely disappeared from the regular market and were sold only on the black market. Despite the celebration of economic growth and the talk of a people's community, income gaps widened and shortages, malnutrition, and related diseases spread among the population. The effect of these nutritional shortcomings can be seen in the overall decline of public health.[9] Mortality rates increased in the mid-1930s and children's heights—used as an indicator of the quality of nutrition and health—stagnated. This represented a reversal from the 1920s and it also stood in opposition to trends occurring in other European countries.

Tight food resources and the small increase in agricultural productivity worried the economic planners. They were especially concerned about the heavy reliance on food imports and the high level of meat consumption. Even before the war began, the Nazi planners had promoted alternatives to meat—especially to beef, which had to be imported—and suggested changes in eating habits that would make more efficient use of the available domestic resources. The Nazi government launched propagandistic campaigns against "Danish butter, Polish eggs, California fruit,

Argentine meat, Canadian wheat, French wine, tropical fruits" and called for greater "nutritional freedom."[10] Göring urged people to only "eat what the German soil yields us."[11] Instead of white wheat bread, people were encouraged to eat whole-meal (*Vollkorn*) or rye bread since rye could be grown more easily even on poor soil all over Germany. The Nazi planners suggested using *quark*, a dairy product made from soured milk formerly fed to animals, instead of butter or margarine, and quark consumption rose by 60 percent in the 1930s.[12] As a way to minimize waste, fruit was to be eaten unpeeled, and people were encouraged to follow a more "natural" diet.[13]

These appeals to eat more "naturally" and frugally were underscored by the example of Hitler himself who was a vegetarian and famously ate simple meals consisting of "a horrible grey barley broth—with crackers and some butter with Gervais-cheese as pudding."[14] Goebbels allegedly served guests who arrived at his house "a meager dinner of herring with boiled potatoes" in exchange for their ration coupons.[15] But not all Nazi leaders led these exemplary lifestyles. Göring, much to the annoyance of Goebbels, could be seen eating, drinking, and celebrating at his hunting lodges or enjoying elaborate meals in luxury restaurants in Berlin. Göring's extravagances and the corruption that existed among the upper ten thousand of the Nazi administration undermined Goebbels's propaganda with its emphasis on a classless "people's community" (*Volksgemeinschaft*) in which everybody had to cut back and make sacrifices.[16]

In addition to being economical, eating "naturally" had other advantages as well. Nazi planners argued that a more natural diet consisting of domestically grown foods would also be beneficial for the "racial health" of the German people and lead to an increase in fertility. Greater racial fitness would prepare Germans for the demands of war as soldiers, workers, and mothers. Improved overall health was especially important for women as the bearers of the German race. Nutrition was thus considered a public matter and women were told that their "body belongs to the Führer!"[17] The "healthy" connection between "blood and soil" was emphasized as well. Eating fruit from the tropics had allegedly broken "the living currents between blood and soil, to which nutrition also belongs."[18] The promotion of a more natural diet presumed an organic way of farming. Organic or alternative farming methods coupled with the rejection of chemical fertilizer and mechanization, however, stood in opposition to the overall goal of increased agricultural productivity.[19]

Underlying all discussion of food supplies was the promise to advance Germany's "nutritional freedom" (*Lebensmittelfreiheit*) or food autarky. To reach this ambitious goal, the Reich Minister of Food, Richard Walther Darré, and his State Secretary in the Ministry, Herbert Backe, announced the first "battle for production" (*Erzeugungsschlacht*) in November 1934. Similar to Benito Mussolini's 1925 *battaglia del grano* that had successfully focused on increased domestic cultivation of wheat in Italy, the "battle for production" was to stimulate agricultural production at home. Italy's wheat production had increased significantly and six years after the beginning of the campaign, the country covered its domestic demand almost entirely on its own.[20] Backe introduced far-reaching measures to stimulate production in Germany. Chemical fertilizer and agricultural machinery were subsidized, land reclamation along the coasts encouraged, and educational programs started and were aimed at making agricultural production more efficient. The measures also included the close oversight of farms, the expanded production of foods that were in short supply, and other economic regulations. The "battle for production" demanded hard labor from the peasants who were expected to make sacrifices "for the nation."[21]

Despite the propagandistic and economic campaigns, domestic production could not be raised significantly during the 1930s. A record harvest in 1933 was followed by a 25 percent fall in rye and wheat the following year.[22] Shortages in grain diminished the availability of fodder and consequently the number of cattle. A bread crisis in 1935–1936 even brought about reminiscences of World War I. With the economic recovery in the industrial sector came the pressure of producing more food, a demand that could not be met with domestic resources. Steady mechanization increased the efficiency of agricultural labor—between 1933 and 1938 the number of tractors increased by 185 percent and the number of harvesters by 50 percent—but the ongoing exodus from the countryside to urban and industrial centers caused a labor shortage. Investment in agriculture went up from 785 million Reichsmark to 988 million Reichsmark (1938), an increase of 25.8 percent.[23] But still, overall agricultural production grew by less than 10 percent—not enough to cover the deficit.[24] Domestic production accounted for 81 percent of the total demand for food in 1933, and the number did not change significantly over the next years.[25] The deficit in fats actually increased, and in 1936 more than half (59.4 percent) of the fats consumed in Germany had to be imported.[26] Despite the emphasis on food autarky, 18.4 percent of the domestic consumption of grain had to be brought in from outside Germany's borders.

Achieving greater nutritional freedom remained a constantly high priority throughout the Third Reich. Since the existing territory did not yield enough food, the solution was to be found in territorial expansion. The quest for more *Lebensraum*, or living space, became the foremost goal. In a secret memo from August 1936, Hitler stated that more *Lebensraum* was needed to increase the available resources and to make Germany self-sufficient for the next war.[27] The plan was to create a greater economic zone (*Grossraumwirtschaft*) that would reorganize continental Europe's markets according to German needs. Grains would come from Southeastern and Eastern Europe, fur from the Baltic countries, and butter would be delivered to Germany from Denmark. During the same year, the first Four-Year Plan was launched with economic reforms that were to increase self-sufficiency and prepare Germany for war. Soon military preparation and industrial production took priority over all other economic questions. "Cannons" had become more important than "bread and butter."[28]

FOOD RATIONING DURING THE WAR

The beginning of the war initially improved Germany's food supplies. Trade shifted from overseas to neighboring countries and occupied territories. Germany enforced favorable trade relations and quickly started to seize food from the places it had invaded. In 1939, Germany was also better prepared for war than in 1914. Having learned the earlier harsh lesson, a complex food-rationing system had been designed before the outbreak of war that would keep a food crisis at bay.

Food rationing started on August 27, 1939, a few days before the attack on Poland.[29] The system was highly differentiated and flexible. All consumers were placed into groups according to their occupation, age, and special needs. By the end of the war, there were sixteen different consumer categories. Each group was allocated a certain amount of calories. The categories encompassed normal consumers, workers engaged in heavy physical work, night workers, and other workers' groups. About one-third of the German population was classified as self-supporting and was thus not included in the rationing system. The members of this group kept their own pigs and other small animals and grew food in their own gardens. Lactating mothers, sick people, elderly persons, and children received special rations. In this carefully designed system, rations were even allocated for dogs![30] Foreign workers made up another category and their rations were calculated based on their nationality. Racial considerations were clearly used in determining the amount of food that was deemed enough. Those regarded as nonproductive and "racially undesirable" did not have the same right to food. Jews were only allowed to buy food at specially designed stores and during limited hours. Jews still living in Germany in 1942 received no meat, eggs, or whole milk, and pregnant Jewish women were excluded from the special allowances reserved for gentile women.[31]

Germans belonging to the German people's community (*Volksgemeinschaft*) were allocated calories according to the consumer group to which they belonged. The rations were adjusted every four weeks to account for emergencies and other life changes. On holidays or special occasions, additional rations were given out. People registered with a local shop and the store received food items according to the number of shoppers that had signed up. Consumers would bring their ration cards, and the shopkeeper collected the coupons and money in exchange for the food items.

The first rationed items included bacon, butter, sugar, meat, tea, cooking fats, and milk. Ration cards allowed consumers to buy a certain amount of designated food items, while other foods could be acquired by means of a point system. The first ration cards allocated 700 grams of meat per week for a normal consumer, 350 grams of fat, 280 grams of sugar, 110 grams of jam, 63 grams of coffee, 150 grams of cereal products (*Nährmittel*), and 60 grams of milk products. For some people—42 percent of the working-class families—these rations actually meant more food than they had had before, since it "equalized" food distribution across the social classes. Special allowances ensured that some families with several children had, for example, more sugar than they needed and could thus trade it for other foods.[32]

A rationing period was valid for four weeks. Adjustment could be made for the next period and the system thus allowed for flexibility and quick responses to changing needs. If a family's home was bombed or a baby was born, rations could be adjusted. People who did not have storage for potatoes, for example, were allowed extra rations.[33] These special accommodations and the built-in flexibility of the system made it more palatable for consumers. Some consumers questioned the placement into certain categories, while shopkeepers tried to get more customers assigned to their stores, but overall the rationing system was readily accepted and considered fair. Goebbels noted the following triumphantly in his diary on September 11, 1940: "Report by Darré on food situation. Things are better than expected and also no worries for the coming year."[34]

Despite the widespread acceptance of food rationing, the system was not without its problems. Since food still had to be purchased, some consumers could not afford it although they had the proper ration card. Prices for food had increased, and shortages of certain items continued. Problems also occurred in the supply and distribution of goods. In other cases, the quality of the products was low and consumers complained, for example, about the watery butter. The caps on prices caused farmers or shopkeepers to withhold food for customers who could pay with something extra. People had to wait in long queues in front of stores and conflicts broke out frequently.[35] Another source of contention was that members of the army, including soldiers who were stationed at home or who were on leave, received considerably higher rations than the normal consumers and could feed their families better. For Christmas, for example, soldiers who were home from the front received special Führer packets, or *Führerpakete*, that contained food items such as flour, sugar, dry cereal, butter, and meat.

A constant concern was the supply of meat and bread. In April 1940, Herbert Backe had little choice but to cut meat rations, and he did so again the following year. In the summer of 1941, the amount of meat available to a normal consumer had shrunk to 400 grams, just a little more than half of the amount of the first ration introduced in August 1939. Nineteen forty-one also saw the beginning of potato rationing. When hopes for a quick victory in the East evaporated and advances on the Russian front stalled, the food situation deteriorated further. Alarmed by a bad harvest and increasing shortages in manpower and food, Nazi economic planners feared a repetition of World War I. A sweet treat for Christmas—everybody received 125 grams of marzipan—was to camouflage the shortages and brighten the mood.[36] Goebbels's worries about how reduced rations would affect the morale of the people led to the government's explicit directive to do anything to avoid further reductions in food allocations to Germans. Taking as many resources as possible from the occupied countries became the highest priority.

But it would only get worse in the following months. More ration cuts were introduced in February 1942, reductions that left the normal consumer with only 300 grams of bread. The situation remained socially explosive.[37] Darré's optimism had been misplaced, and he would pay for this with his job. His ongoing conflicts with Göring over food rations culminated in his removal from his ministerial position in spring 1942. He was officially put on medical leave since the regime did not want to create the impression that problems in food supplies had demanded a change in leadership. Herbert Backe, the administrator of the efficient food-rationing system, had long gained the confidence of Göring and Hitler, and took over his former boss's portfolio.[38] Backe's main concern remained the supply of food, and in his mind only the ruthless exploitation of the occupied territories in the East could alleviate the situation.[39]

The war—while supposedly launched to bring bread and employment to Germans—greatly hampered agricultural production and quickly diminished food reserves. The military draft and new opportunities in the expanding war industries led to a serious shortage of farm labor. The workload for those who stayed in the countryside dramatically increased. Farmers' wives and daughters remained on the farm while their husbands and brothers left for the front or for better paying industrial jobs. Rationalization and investment in agriculture slowed down since the demands of the war economy gave priority to armaments production. Since horses were requisitioned for the war effort as well, fewer draft animals were available to help with the hard labor on the farm. Fuel shortages, the lack of spare parts, and shortages in artificial fertilizer further affected agricultural output. Agricultural production did not keep up with the overall economic growth, and a more radical solution had to be found to meet German nutritional needs.

FOOD POLICY AS RACIAL POLICY

One way to redistribute tight food resources was to employ food rationing as a tool to get rid of those who were unwanted. During the so-called euthanasia program, Nazi doctors killed thousands of patients in hospitals and institutions after declaring them incurably sick. The "euthanasia" program had begun in fall 1939 and aimed at killing people the Nazis considered "unworthy of life"—people with psychiatric or physical disabilities and who were considered a burden to German society. A "merciful death" was granted to probably as many as two hundred thousand mentally or physically handicapped people.[40] How many of them—and how many more—were slowly murdered by receiving an insufficient amount of food is largely unknown. At a conference held by the Bavarian Interior Ministry in November 1942 for directors of mental hospitals, the doctors were asked to formulate a special diet for incurably ill patients. A directive followed on November 30 ordering the directors to immediately institute these special diets in their respective hospitals.[41] Several doctors followed up enthusiastically. In the asylum of Kaufbeuren, for example, the director Dr. Valentin Faltlhauser designed a diet for his patients consisting of potatoes, yellow turnips, and boiled cabbage, foods almost devoid of fats and protein. The intended effect, according to Faltlhauser—who also was a consultant for the euthanasia program and made lists of patients destined for death—was a "slow death, which should ensue in about three months."[42] Under Dr. Faltlhauser's directive, 1,200 to 1,600 patients—including 210 children—were murdered in Kaufbeuren.

Strong racism was also displayed in Nazi food propaganda. The regime circulated reports about starving workers in Great Britain and in the United States and blamed the Western Allies for having brought hunger to Germany. "The Russians" took the brunt of the bad propaganda. They appeared as insatiably hungry, greedy, and bestial in their eating manners. Their land was the most fertile in Europe, but the alleged inability to farm successfully had created domestic shortages and hunger at home.[43] Nazi propaganda emphasized that Russia was unable to feed its own people and that the Communist regime had brought mass starvation to its own country. If unrestrained, Russia would also bring hunger to Germany. While racism was employed in the food propaganda against other Slavic people as well, Jews and Soviet citizens took the brunt of the hatred and were prohibited from eating any "German bread."[44]

German agricultural production, however, depended heavily on the labor of these "racially inferior" people. In Prussia in September 1939, for example, one hundred thousand Polish POWs had helped bring in the potato harvest. By 1941, 1.3 million Polish and Ukrainian forced laborers were employed in Germany, in addition to more than one million French and Soviet POWs. It has been estimated that foreign laborers forced to work for Germany produced approximately 20 percent of the food grown in Germany during the war.[45]

The absence of German men and the presence of large numbers of foreign laborers in the midst of German families increased the Nazis' racial concerns. Since Slavic laborers were considered to be racially inferior, official regulations advised Germans to be cautious when interacting with them. They were to keep their distance and let the foreign laborers know that they were not equal.

By law, foreign laborers had to wear letters on their clothes to distinguish them from German laborers, their pay was miniscule and they were not allowed to socialize with Germans or eat with them at the same table. In the countryside, however, these laws were sometimes ignored. A wide range of relationships existed between peasants and forced laborers, and sometimes the forced laborers were well fed and well integrated into the farm family—in contrast to forced laborers in industry who faced horrendous conditions.[46] Practical considerations thus subverted the Nazis racial food hierarchy so carefully designed.

Over the years, the demand for foreign laborers increased. In 1942, thirty-four thousand foreign workers were brought to Germany every week. In the summer of 1943, 6.5 million toiled in German factories or on farms,[47] and 4.95 million of these were civilians, not captured soldiers.[48] In the fall of 1944, the number of foreign workers in Germany rose to 7.9 million—or more than 20 percent of the workforce. Until spring 1941, many of the forced laborers had been from France, but in 1942 the focus of military campaigns shifted to Eastern Europe. This shift came along with major changes in the treatment of the prisoners. While Germany had largely followed the Geneva Convention of 1929 that regulated how POWs were to be treated, these conventions were not followed when dealing with captured soldiers on the Eastern front. Clear racial hatred determined the "planning"—or absence thereof—for taking prisoners from Poland or the Soviet Union. No adequate camps were set up to house the millions of captured soldiers; they were treated harshly and often killed on the spot and the completely inadequate food rations led to hunger and mass starvation.[49] Those who were sent to Germany to work on farms faced horrendous living and working conditions as well.

The Nazis understood that the prisoners had to eat to work for Germany, and thus the Nazi planners searched for ever cheaper ways of feeding them. The Reich Ministry of Food funded scientific studies that examined the connection between nutrition and increased physical efficiency.[50] The Institute for the Physiology of Labor did extensive research on the number of calories needed for a variety of jobs, the impact of glucose on workers' performance, and on attempts to expand every gram of food as efficiently as possible using foreign workers as the focus of the study.[51] Scientists discovered that it was more effective to feed one worker 3,000 calories a day than giving two workers 1,500 calories each. Research showed that if two workers were given 1,500 calories a day, they would use up all their energy simply to stay alive. A well-fed worker who received 3,000 calories could spend the extra energy on productive labor. However, since it was not feasible to increase the rations for foreign laborers while at the same time cutting rations for German civilians, ideological concerns overruled these newly discovered practical considerations and foreign workers received rations that were often not enough to survive on.

The experimentation with inexpensive ways to feed the foreign laborers knew few limits. Heinrich Himmler, the leader of the SS and General Plenipotentiary for the entire administration of the Reich, promoted a newly invented sausage that was made from waste products of cellulose production. Flavored with liver aroma, it apparently looked and smelled like liver sausage. Himmler described the "sausage" as "unbelievably nourishing, tasty, sausage-like paste, that made excellent foodstuff."[52] This so-called sausage was given to inmates at the Mauthausen concentration camp. When an inmate secretly examined the food under a microscope he discovered that it was crawling with bacteria. Stomach and intestinal disorders killed 116 prisoners in Mauthausen alone. Nonetheless, the sausage continued to be produced and was also given to prisoners in the Dachau, Buchenwald, and Sachsenhausen concentration camps. Another example of a special food designed to feed Soviet prisoners working in Germany was the so-called Russian bread. The German Ministry of Food advised its bakers on November 24, 1941, to make a bread from "a useful mixture consisting of 50 percent rye bran, 20 percent residue of sugar beet, 20 percent cellulose flour and 10 percent flour made of straw or leaves."[53]

While the poor quality of the food and the small size of the rations allocated to foreign laborers were enough to kill many of them, the horrendous working conditions in the factories and mines added to the death count. Half of the 1.95 million Soviet POWs employed in Germany after November 1941 died. Altogether, a total of nearly seven million Jewish and non-Jewish workers were killed in Germany.[54] The racial dimension of Nazi food policy becomes clear by comparing the death rate among Soviet captured soldiers and soldiers taken in German captivity on the Western front. While more than 50 percent of the Soviet POWs died, "only" 4 percent of the Western POWs were killed. French and British soldiers were treated better and received greater food rations than the Soviets or Poles who fell into German hands.[55]

HUNGER IN GERMANY, 1944–1945

The experience of hunger, however, would also come to Germans at home. The food supply system held out until the last winter of the war. By that time, British and American bombs had destroyed cities and infrastructures, the losses on the front had become undeniable, and food was increasingly difficult to come by. The reduction of potato rations brought the turnip back onto the table with all its memories of World War I. Strict government controls tried to prevent chaos in food distribution, but could do little to stop the spread of hunger and desperation. People rushed to the stores to buy up the few items available—hoarding or *Hamsterkäufe* became commonplace. They illegally slaughtered animals and bartered what they could on the black market to secure enough food. Since prices for food had remained low while prices for other items had gone up, it was much more lucrative for agricultural producers to sell their produce on the black market.

The Nazi government had introduced close oversight of agricultural production, but the prominence of small-scale farming made it hard for the state to control its farmers and what they produced. Farmers and consumers were creative in finding ways to circumvent the rules or simply to use tricks to acquire the necessary food. They failed to register their livestock, cheated on the report cards or kept meat to be sold illegally. Consumers swapped and traded everything from coffee to sugar, used connections, or smuggled food. Overall, the state could not exercise total control, and even draconian laws helped little to force consumers to follow the rules or bring farmers to deliver their food. Many small peasants simply withdrew from the market, fed their families, and scaled back their production.[56]

By the last winter of the war, the food supply system had finally collapsed. The advancing enemy forces had drastically diminished the availability of food. Soldiers had been ordered to feed themselves off the enemy land, but no plans were made for a scenario in which Germany would lose these territories. Backe described these problems in his August 1944 report and noted that the continuous support of the troops put great pressure on food supplies. He ordered that all special allowances be cut and army rations reduced to the level of civilian rations. Food deliveries from Serbia and other allies had to be increased. A stricter control of farm production was to account for even the last domestic resources. In his annual report about the food situation, Backe's tone was cautious: "the less desirable factors outweigh the favorable factors for an acceptable or good harvest."[57] Even after the ration adjustments, the food situation remained critical. The draft of all men, including the old, very young, and those who previously had been considered indispensable, further increased the shortage of labor. Fields remained uncultivated and the grain was not threshed. The ongoing deficiencies in fuel, fertilizer, and machinery limited agricultural production. The destruction of railroads, bridges, and roads hindered transportation and the collapse of infrastructure only added to the catastrophic situation.[58]

To improve the distribution of scarce resources, Backe introduced more changes to the ration system in fall 1944. Instead of separate cards for each food item, "basic cards" (*Grundkarten*) were given out that could be applied to different foods. The desperate measure did little to improve the situation and Backe admitted defeat in January 1945. Rations could not be secured until the next harvest. He introduced temporary adjustments to the rations, but no end date was given for the reductions. Hitler, who had denied any signs of a crisis and had not wanted to hear of ration cuts, finally caved in. Rations of sugar, bread, meat, and fats were reduced for all consumer categories. Available calories per person had diminished by almost half compared to the situation at the beginning of the war.[59] The rations had become so small that a hunger crisis was imminent.

At the end of the war in May 1945, the victorious Allies faced a daunting task. All over Europe, millions of displaced persons, liberated prisoners, refugees, and expellees needed emergency aid from the Allied occupation powers, but the total collapse of infrastructure, agricultural production, and industry exacerbated the situation. For Germany, the redrawn borders established at the Potsdam Conference meant the loss of agricultural territories to the east (especially East Prussia) that had been critical for the production of food. To alleviate the critical situation, the Allies kept the agrarian apparatus in place that had been established under the Nazis. Backe genuinely thought the Allies would need his expertise to deal with the food crisis; he was thus "surprised" when he was taken prisoner and ended up in Nuremberg to be tried as a war criminal.[60]

Despite the extent of the crisis, the Western Allies secured the survival of millions of Germans and food supplies started to improve relatively quickly. The end of the rationing system came when aid from the U.S. Marshall Plan started to pour into West Germany in early 1948. Later that year, the Western Allies also instituted a currency reform that instantly filled store shelves with food. By the 1950s, West Germans had so much to eat again that the recovery seemed indeed "miraculous."[61] The economic recovery in the eastern part of the country took much longer. The Soviet Occupied Zone was excluded from Marshall aid, and a hastily implemented land reform impacted agricultural production negatively. The collectivization of agriculture accelerated in the second half of the 1950s. By the mid-1960s all arable land in East Germany was incorporated into collectives or state farms.[62]

In early 1945, however, the end to food shortages still seemed like a distant dream all over Germany. As alternate food sources, Nazi publications offered tips on how to use tree bark, saw dust, and chestnuts in food preparation or how to catch frogs for a meal.[63] Peasants were urged to make sacrifices and to give "bread to the soldiers and workers" and seemed to live up to these expectations.[64] An American observer described the peasants as "busily cultivating the fields and preparing to try to feed the millions of refugees from the east now within the shrunken homeland."[65] No major disturbances, resistance, or conflicts among producers and consumers seem to have occurred. People continued to work, did what was necessary to stay alive, and followed directions until the very end. Ensuring food and survival in addition to processing the political news and the mounting number of losses required all the energy that was left.[66]

Overall, Germany's food policy during World War II accomplished its goals. Germans had to adjust their eating habits and make do with substitute food as well as deal with shortages. The overall calories available per consumer per day diminished from 2,400 to 2,000 in fall 1944, but this was still high enough to keep people alive and functioning.[67] Compared to World War I, the ration system worked better; it provided nuanced and generally satisfactory rations for German consumers; and most importantly, it did not pit German consumer groups against each other. The question of food and hunger thus fueled, rather than eroded, the popular support of the Nazi war. Agricultural production was kept going despite the urgencies of the war economy. Last but not least, the ruthless exploitation of occupied territories allowed Germans to have enough to eat, while hunger was shifted to other groups on a mass scale. The foremost victims of German food policy were Jews, foreign workers from Eastern Europe and the Soviet Union, and the internees in the ghettos and concentration camps.

3

HERBERT BACKE AT THE CENTER OF FOOD POLITICS

Given the centrality of food politics and economic planning, it is not surprising that the men in the Reich Ministry of Food and Agriculture gained substantial political clout. The power structure within the Nazi regime was polycratic; responsibilities of departments and officials often overlapped and power hierarchies were not always linear. Bureaucrats and higher-level administrators consequently could take on roles that gave them great influence and allowed them to make decisions without following the flowchart of formal command. One of these men was Herbert Backe (1896–1947), state secretary in Richard Walther Darré's Reich Ministry, food commissioner in the Four-Year Plan administration and later Reich Minister. Backe's rapid rise from failed academic to influential food minister and close confidant of Adolf Hitler, Hermann Göring, and Heinrich Himmler demonstrates the role food and food politics played in the Nazi regime.

Backe's life and his political career in the Reich Food Ministry are an interesting case study of a Nazi leader. Backe was born to German émigrés in the southwestern corner of the Russian Empire and spent the first twenty years of his life in the Caucasus region. The outbreak of World War I put an abrupt end to his family's relatively comfortable life in Russia. Backe was arrested and interned in a small village in the Ural Mountains for several years, and he only arrived in Germany in summer 1918 after a hazardous escape from Russia. In the 1920s he rebuilt his life, earned a university degree in agriculture, and leased a farm in northern Germany. In the early 1930s, his political career took off. Backe and Darré worked together to push through some major agricultural legislation in the first years of the Nazi regime, but their relationship became increasingly adversarial. Darré felt more and more shut out by the closed circle of Nazi leaders and by his former protégé, even though his ideas continued to be employed and would remain pillars of Nazi ideology until the final collapse of the regime. Backe turned out to be the more capable administrator who helped prepare Germany for war and introduced a well-functioning ration system that sustained Germans for most of the war. Backe's expertise made him the man of choice for Hitler to plan the economic aspects of the Operation Barbarossa and to organize the exploitation of the Soviet Union.[1]

The "Russia expert" among the Nazi leaders, Backe's racial hatred for the very people he grew up with was rooted in his experiences following the outbreak of World War I. He issued repeated warnings not to show any sympathy with Soviet citizens and his disdain for "the Russians" would later influence the decisions over their fate during the Barbarossa campaign. Under Backe's leadership, civilians succumbed to hunger in Soviet cities and more than two million Soviet prisoners of war died of starvation in German captivity. If Backe had had it his way, tens of millions of Russian civilians would have fallen victim to the same fate. Only the failure of the Barbarossa campaign and the impracticality of Backe's *Hungerplan* ("hunger plan") prevented this from happening on an even larger scale. While the fate of Soviet citizens and soldiers and the connection between food policy and genocide are the topics of the next chapter, this chapter looks at the life, career, and political ideas of Herbert Backe, the man at the center of Nazi food politics and food distribution during the Third Reich.

RUSSIAN ROOTS

Backe was born on May 1, 1896, in Batumi, a city on the shores of the Black Sea in Georgia, a region that had been annexed by the Russian Empire in the nineteenth century. Its location on the peripheries of the Russian, Ottoman, and Persian empires had made the area the center of political, religious, and military rivalries throughout history and continues to be in the news about regional territorial disputes after the collapse of the Soviet Union. Its population consisted of more than fifty different ethnic groups with their own cultures, languages, and religious beliefs. Backe's maternal ancestors, the Wetzel family, were originally from Württemberg, but the family had immigrated to southwestern Russia and settled in the Caucasus region at the beginning of the nineteenth century. In exchange for free land and the release from taxes and military service, many German settlers decided to leave their homeland and ventured out upon this hazardous journey.[2] In Russia, his mother's family had shed their peasant roots and owned a successful brewery in Tiflis. On a family trip to Germany in 1891—her first trip outside the Caucasus—Louise Wetzel met Albrecht Backe. According to their daughter Hortense's recollections, it was love at first sight. Albrecht and Louise married in October 1892, and their first child Helmut (a twin brother died soon after birth) was born in July 1893.[3] Herbert was born in 1896, followed by three sisters, Hedwig (1898), Herta (1900), and Hortense (1903).

After the father's agricultural machinery business in Odessa had folded, the family moved to Tiflis. According to the recollections of Herbert's sister Hortense, their upbringing in the Russian Empire was filled with happy childhood moments together with members of their extended family. Grandfather Wetzel had bought a piece of land in Kodjori, a resort town outside of Tiflis and well known for its healthy air. Many middle-class families had their weekend homes, or *datschas*, in Kodjori. Wetzel built several houses on the property for his children; one of them would later be occupied by Louise and her family (after her husband's death). In Kodjori, the children played in the woods, went hunting, played with friends, went sledding, and admired the customs and traditions of the Grusinier (Georgian) people. Herbert attended a German Protestant elementary school in Tiflis and moved to a Russian school after third grade. The political and economic crisis after the 1905 Revolution, followed by personal tragedies—Grandfather Wetzel died and Herbert's father committed suicide in 1907—shook the foundation of the family's well-being. Despite the economic difficulties, Herbert Backe and his sister Hortense would later describe their youth in Russia as a happy time in their life.[4]

Life for the German community in Russia changed profoundly with the outbreak of World War I. Speaking German in public was outlawed, and German customs such as the brewing of beer became illegal. Children were forced to leave Russian schools and German men were taken into custody. Herbert's youth came to an abrupt end in September 1914 when he was imprisoned and sent to a small village in the Urals.[5] Herbert became very ill, but refused to go home without the release of a friend who was also held prisoner. He was consequently transferred to the even smaller and more distant village Vjatka, where he lived without any contact to his family for years.[6] Herbert remained in custody until his escape from the village when he made it all the way to St. Petersburg, crossing the country by foot and train. The Swedish consulate in St. Petersburg helped Herbert emigrate and he arrived in Germany in June 1918.

Backe was part of a generation of young German men who came to adulthood during the years of war and revolution, and their disappointment with the Versailles peace treaty was followed by great disillusionment with the young democratic republic. These men felt isolated, frustrated, and helpless in the face of the political turmoil, social collapse, and economic decline around them. They wanted to take matters into their own hands and channeled their energy into the emerging radical political groups and paramilitary organizations that promised to do something about the crisis. Backe's own path followed this pattern. His family's dramatic social and economic decline, his personal hardships, and the sudden end to his childhood left their mark on the young man, who later acknowledged that imprisonment, political chaos, and degradation were instrumental to his lifelong interest in social and economic questions. His personal experiences also hardened his feelings of nationalism. It embittered him that he and his family, who had worked so hard to climb up the social ladder in their new homeland had lost everything and were regarded as enemies by a country that had been their home, "just because they were German."[7] Like so many other Nazi leaders, his ideological anti-bolshevism and political nationalism had its roots in this period of dramatic change and political turmoil.

In the 1920s, Backe developed a vision that would resonate with the Nazis' worldview. He promoted a new era of economic organization that would overcome the crisis caused by liberalism, the free market, and the rule of the bourgeoisie. This new economic system would secure national food supplies and was built upon a foundation of peasant farmers. Backe considered peasants to be the source of Germany's racial vitality who had to be protected from the destructive forces of liberalism. Backe's ideas reverberated with the Nazis' sense of historic mission to reorganize the market relations and food distribution of continental Europe. His vision was radical and looked to the future, rather than aiming at restoring an ideal peasant economy of the past. At the same time it was highly critical of Britain and its embodiment of imperialism, parliamentarianism, and liberalism. According to Backe, global markets had destroyed self-sufficient peasant farms, and the monopolies of grain, meat, and dairy production had replaced the great diversity of peasant farming. This, however, had not made the world's food supplies any more secure. While food was produced on a massive scale, famine and food insecurities had not disappeared. The global interdependence of food markets had led to the great agrarian crises of the late 1920s and had hit farmers especially hard. The only way to solve the problems of the time, according to Backe, was through a radical transformation of the economic system. Germany would lead the reorganization of continental Europe.[8]

Backe's critique of Britain had strong racist overtones. He regarded capitalism and liberalism as the product of Jewish influence. Like other conservative and agrarian ideologists, he considered Germany's shortage of land (as compared to the number of farmers) to be the most significant limitation to Germany's power (*Volk ohne Raum* or "people without space"). Measured by land available per farmer, Germany was in fact more similar to "peasant nations" such as Ireland or Bulgaria rather than other industrial powers.[9] The distribution of land within Germany seemed unfavorable for Germany's economic development. A very small number of larger landowners—less than 1 percent—dominated one-quarter of the agricultural land, while three-quarters of the farms were small holdings with 0.5 to 10 hectares of land. Larger peasant farms of 10 to 100 hectares made up only about one-quarter of all farms and 43 percent of the available farmland.[10] For most German peasants, farming the land was hard labor with little profit. They depended on family labor and incomes had to be supplemented with other lines of work. German conservative thinkers had long lamented the "flight from the countryside" (*Landflucht*), but little could be done to stop the trend. According to many, the greatest shortcoming was that Germany did not have enough space to provide land for all farmers and to produce enough food for all German people. Germany was heavily dependent on the import of food, a fact that could make it vulnerable during times of conflict.

This is where the agrarian ideology met Nazi ideology. Hitler's plans for conquest in the East would provide the "space" the agrarian visionaries wanted. The reorganization of continental Europe under German leadership would solve the food crisis, with a clear division of labor and racial hierarchy. Backe foresaw an economic transformation led by a new leadership class that did not consist of the "inferior Russians," but of precisely the people without space, the Germans. Large-scale German settlement in the East implied a major demographic reorganization of peoples living in the territory, and it envisioned the subordination, enslavement, and mass murder of people deemed inferior. Herbert Backe, Richard Walther Darré, Heinrich Himmler, and Adolf Hitler all shared this vision of conquest and colonization.[11]

THE BEGINNING OF BACKE'S POLITICAL INVOLVEMENT

The Backe family reunited in Germany after the war, but the 1920s continued to be years of economic hardships and social dislocation for the elderly mother and her four children. Herbert's brother had to discontinue his studies in engineering for financial reasons, and his sister dropped out of her studies in art and had to earn money as a seamstress (*Schneiderin*). His other two sisters worked as domestic servants for very little money, while their mother was sickly and dependent on the care from her children. At the same time, however, the 1920s were years when Herbert turned things around for himself and his family. He took on a variety of day jobs and finished his high school degree. Among other things, he worked as a farm hand for eight months near Hanover, an experience that marked the beginning of his commitment to agriculture and determined his political career. After registering for classes at Göttingen University, he finished his studies in six semesters with a degree in agriculture. His first job after graduation was on a farm near Eschwege in Lower Saxony, where he received room and board and one hundred pounds of rye for pay. He continued his academic studies as an assistant to Professor Erich Obst in agricultural geography (*Agrargeographie*) at Hanover Technical University in 1924 and organized study trips to Russia for the professor and his students. Backe's knowledge of the Russian language and agriculture made him a good candidate for the position, and it secured him a modest monthly income (200 *Reichsmark*). The family also received some compensation for their losses in Russia. In 1926, his brother picked up his studies to finish his degree in engineering, and Herbert's two younger sisters trained as a pharmacist and a pediatric nurse. It seemed as if things had changed for the better for the Backe family.[12]

Although Herbert worked on a dissertation thesis to obtain his doctorate, his real passion was practical agricultural work, not academics.[13] He took a modest job on a large farm in Eastern Pommerania (*Hinterpommern*) in the winter of 1926 and was soon given more responsibilities. Less than a year later he started looking for his own land to buy. He became engaged to Ursula Kahl, and with the financial help of his fiancée's father, he leased the run-down estate Domäne Hornsen near Hanover—in the district (*Kreis*) of Alfeld/Leine—in September 1928. The farm would be the family's home for the next twenty years, and even when the Backes moved to Berlin in 1933–1934 because of the father's political post in the Nazi Reich Ministry, the mother and children continued to spend their summers on the farm and finally returned to it in 1943–1944.[14] The timing of the takeover of the farm in the late 1920s was unfortunate because of the looming agrarian crisis. Prices for agricultural products plummeted and hit bottom after the worldwide crash in 1929. Nevertheless, Herbert and Ursula Backe made the farm profitable. Backe's own involvement in farm work during the agricultural crisis convinced him that only a radical economic and political change would turn things around.

Backe's first political involvement with the young Nazi circles had occurred while he was enrolled at the University of Göttingen.[15] He had joined the paramilitary organization of the Nazi Party, the SA or "Brownshirts," in 1922 and became a member of the Nazi Party in 1925.[16] Backe's ideas of a "folk community," of a "healthy" corporate society resonated with National Socialist ideology and he believed in Social Darwinist ideas of racial selection. He also shared the Nazis' hatred of communism and liberalism.[17] The leader of his regional Nazi Party branch described Backe as a "strong supporter of racial theory" who was drawn to the "uncompromising toughness and clarity of our struggle."[18] But Backe's involvement in politics was minimal at this point in his life. He was too busy on his own farm to consider political actions, and when his local political district *Gau*, Hannover-Süd (Hanover South), was dissolved, he did not even renew his membership in the Nazi Party. Two decades later, Backe reflected on the beginning of his involvement in politics and his negative view of political parties and political organizations in his "Great Report" (*Grosser Bericht*), his own recollections written while awaiting trial in the Nuremberg prison in 1945. In the "Great Report," he describes how his own "calling" came with the economic crisis in 1929 when he felt it his duty to get involved. He thus reconnected with the Nazi Party and renewed his membership in October 1931.

In spring 1931, Backe heard Hitler speak in front of a large audience in Braunschweig, an event that would transform his political engagement. He later reflected on how he had admired Hitler's ability to "reduce complicated political, cultural and economic developments to short 'primitive' formulas and characterizations that were so much clearer than his enemies' twisted explanations."[19] Backe's second encounter with Hitler in October 1931—at an SA rally in Braunschweig—confirmed his favorable impression. Again, he thought that Hitler, in contrast to the Nazi Party in general (and Backe would make this critical distinction repeatedly in the years to come) was able to propose positive solutions to the big problems of the time. Hitler's appeal to the "folk community," to the idealism and sacrifice of each individual, resonated strongly with Backe. He felt personally called, and this feeling would not leave him until Hitler's death.[20] A year and a half later, Backe described in a letter to his wife how he interpreted the look that Hitler gave him and knew that "this man would force me to fight until the end."[21] Backe kept his promise. In April 1941, he explained to his wife that nobody else understood the Führer the way he did and that the depth of his conviction was greater than anybody else's.[22] Awaiting his trial after the war, Backe further analyzed "his own path to Hitler," a path that "millions of others" took with him.[23]

The way Backe described the effect Hitler's speech had on him is similar to how other people felt when they heard Hitler speak. Albert Speer, Hitler's chief architect and Reich Minister of Armaments and War Production, for example, remarked in his autobiography that after reluctantly attending a political meeting in December 1930 with Hitler as the featured speaker, he was deeply impressed and surprised by Hitler's style and rhetoric. "Hitler had taken hold of him then and had not released him since" was how Speer explained that first encounter.[24] Speer, who had avoided political meetings and groups until then, was taken by Hitler's oratory skills, his skill in evoking the problems of the time, his apocalyptic vision, but also by his confidence and charismatic leadership. Speer, just like Backe, walked away from his first encounter with Hitler as a changed man and soon after he joined the "Hitler Party" on March 1, 1931.

In late 1931, Backe ran for an office on the Nazi Party's ticket and became chair of the local peasant organization in Hanover, the *Hannoverscher Landbund*. It was during this time that Richard Walther Darré took notice of Backe. Darré had read one of Backe's articles published in a National Socialist newspaper and liked his point of view on the contradictions between peasant agriculture and the world economy. Darré invited Backe to Munich to attend the election of *Reichspräsident* in early 1932, where Backe met Darré and Hitler. Darré took on the role of a political mentor to Backe and convinced him to run for the Prussian parliament. Backe's campaign was successful and he joined parliament in April 1932, only to realize how much he disliked parliamentary politics. He thought that "nothing got done" and complained about the "hollowness of German parliamentarianism."[25] In early January 1933, Backe was charged to report directly to Hitler about Germany's agricultural issues; Backe had become a member of Hitler's close circle and would be at the epicenter of decision making for the years to come. Hitler's respect for Backe's expertise and skills as a food administrator would only grow over the years, and Hitler ultimately appointed him as the man in charge of food policies in Germany and in Operation Barbarossa.[26]

WRITING AGRICULTURAL LEGISLATION: DARRÉ AND BACKE IN THE 1930S

Darré's early mentorship of the young Backe was instrumental to Backe's political success within the Nazi Party. Their professional relationship was complemented by a personal friendship that extended to their families. Backe's wife, Ursula, described in her diary her first positive impressions of Darré, and happily noticed that her children responded well to him.[27] The relationship between her husband and Darré remained a topic of Ursula's diaries throughout the years. The tone—and the relationship itself—changed dramatically—from the well-liked "uncle" Darré who became the godfather to Ursula and Herbert's oldest son, Albrecht,[28] to the pitiful rival with whom Herbert was engaged in a sort of "brotherly battle." The shifting power relationship between the two men illustrates the power struggles within the Nazi regime itself and would determine the path of Nazi food politics.

This analysis of Backe's life and his relationship with Darré is based on some amazing historical documents. Backe did not leave an unusually large number of personal papers in the archives, and compared to other historical figures, his track record measured in meters of archival binders he left behind might not be impressive. However, the kinds of documents left in his collection are remarkable. In addition to the paper record from the political offices and departments he worked for, Backe was an active communicator and letter writer. He regularly wrote to his wife Ursula from Berlin while she stayed with the children on the Hornsen farm near Hanover. Herbert told his wife in detail about his emotions, his frustrations, his impressions of others, and his daily work in general. This information was not lost on his wife, who recorded everything in her diary she kept over the years.[29] These diaries turned out to be an extraordinary source. Ursula Backe wrote with the intention to record "things of great magnitude" that were happening around her. She wrote with a mission and with a purpose, similar to how her husband pursued his job. She had no doubts that her husband and the Nazis were doing the right things, and her support of the party did not end with the collapse of the regime. An early statement in her diary from 1934 is characteristic for her thinking throughout the years:

> Herbert often reads in Hitler's book, and it helped me tremendously in the conversations afterwards in which I gained clarity about a wonderful reason to exist in the future. Until then I hadn't known exactly what kind of life I should wish for or what I should imagine for the children. Now everything is clear. Now I see a long path of struggle that will last for generations and that has a wonderful goal, and all our lives and theirs—and all future life will become part of this vision.[30]

She noticed that her husband was often depressed, frustrated, and physically exhausted. In May 1934, Ursula Backe recorded in her diary that "Herbert is miserable and restless. He has a lot of frustrations at work and finds his job useless."[31] But despite the drawbacks, Herbert never lost his admiration for Hitler and the cause, and he never questioned his ideas. In 1944, when even the most adamant supporters had to acknowledge that the war was lost, Herbert Backe talked to his wife about preparation for the murder of their children.[32] It never came to that, but in the Nuremberg prison awaiting his trial Backe committed suicide. A world without National Socialism was unimaginable for him. The diaries and letters, then, have been of tremendous help in sketching a picture of the man behind the actions in the realm of food policy.[33]

The conflicts between Darré and Backe later on do not diminish the close collaboration between the two men in the 1930s. Initially, it was Darré who had been charged by Hitler to rally the peasantry behind the Nazis.[34] Darré was already well known in "folkish" (*völkisch*) circles for his publications on agriculture, animal breeding, and racial theories. Just like Backe, Darré's life had begun outside Germany. He was born in 1895 to German parents in Argentina. When Darré was nine years old, his parents sent him to Germany to attend school in Heidelberg; the rest of his family followed seven years later. He served in World War I and worked as a farm assistant in Pommerania for a few years after the war. In 1922, he picked up his academic studies—he had never finished high school before the war—and enrolled at the University of Halle to study agronomy and zoology with a special focus on animal breeding. He received his master's degree in 1925 and his doctorate in 1929. In the late 1920s, Darré worked in agricultural administration and published extensively on livestock selection and its application to human beings. His writings and way of thinking were heavily indebted to racial theories. Darré's two books, *The Peasantry as the Life-Source of the Nordic Race* (*Das Bauerntum als Lebensquell der nordischen Rasse*, 1929) and *New Nobility from Blood and Soil* (*Neuadel aus Blut und Boden*, 1930), made his name well known in right-wing intellectual circles. He was an active member in the Artaman League, a youth group that promoted conservative back-to-the-land and nationalistic ideas closely related to Nazi ideology, and a member of the paramilitary organization *Stahlhelm* that was associated with the conservative German National People's Party (DNVP). In the Artaman League he met another future Nazi leader, Heinrich Himmler, who became an early supporter of Darré. The two men shared a passion for agrarian questions and the ancient mystical history of Germanic tribes. Darré was introduced to Hitler at a social gathering organized by his publisher Julius Friedrich Lehmann in 1930. Apparently Hitler had heard of Darré and his publications on racial theory and his experience in agricultural administration.[35] Soon after the meeting, Hitler commissioned Darré to organize the countryside and bring existing peasant associations in line with the Nazi Party. In 1931, Darré became the director of Himmler's new SS Race and Settlement Office (*Rasse- und Siedlungshauptamt*, RuSHA) that oversaw the "marriage order" for SS personnel and promoted racial policies.[36] Darré remained in this position until Himmler replaced him with Günther Pancke in 1938. By that time, Darré's personal friendship with Himmler had vanished, but the connections the two men had made between the SS, agrarian ideology and racial policies were there to stay. It was Backe who continued in Darré's footsteps and helped Himmler implement the murderous policies that followed from these agrarian theories.[37]

Hitler had picked the right person for the task to "coordinate" the countryside. Darré successfully "united" all agricultural interest groups, a great accomplishment considering how bitterly divided these interest groups had been before and during World War I. In the Weimar Republic the dream of a united "green front" that could give German agriculture one voice in the struggle against urban and industrial interests had become even less attainable because of the agricultural crisis that had hit many farmers hard and had radicalized their interest organizations. This rivalry among agrarian interest groups made it easier for Darré to infiltrate the existing interest groups, and he used the familiar Nazi tactics of discrediting other political parties, open intimidation, and terror against peasant leaders to silence dissenting voices.[38]

To keep the countryside in line, Darré created a powerful new organization, the Agrarian Apparatus (*Agrarpolitischer Apparat*) that controlled all farmers' associations and reached every village in the Reich through appointed and carefully selected party officials.[39] One official proudly announced that there was

> no farm, no estate, no village, no cooperative, no agricultural industry, no local organization of the RLB [*Reichs-Landbund*, the main agrarian interest organization in the 1920s], no rural equestrian association, etc., where we have not—at the least—placed our LVL [*Landwirtschaftliche Vertrauensleute*, or "agrarian agents"] in such numbers that we could paralyze at one blow the total political life of these structures.[40]

Agrarian organizers held countless peasant meetings and rural folks were reached through targeted propaganda material. The *Nationalsozialistische Landpost*, a news magazine published from 1931 to 1945, addressed a variety of peasant issues and remained a powerful propaganda tool throughout the years.[41] By late 1932, Darré could proudly claim that the countryside had been successfully organized and brought in line with the Nazi Party. The electoral support for the Nazis was especially high in the rural areas of northern and eastern Germany, where Hitler received a majority of the votes.

In recognition of his achievements in the rural sector, Hitler named Darré Reich Peasant Leader (*Reichsbauernführer*) in May 1933 and appointed him as the new Reich Minister of Food and Agriculture in June of the same year. Darré had reached the height of his political career. He was a well-published writer on racial theories and a powerful political organizer in the countryside, and he had now become the head of the agricultural ministry. He had entered the circle of political elite in the Nazi regime. In October of the same year, Darré appointed Backe as his deputy (*Staatssekretär*, or state secretary). Together, these two men would make "blood and soil" one of the pillars of Nazi ideology. They worked closely together and introduced some major changes in agrarian policy that would be in place for the remainder of the "Thousand-Year Reich."

Most importantly, Darré and Backe created a new organization, the Reich Food Estate (*Reichsnährstand*, or RNS), that would control the entire food sector, from agricultural production to marketing and consumption. It was a mass organization that consisted of more than seventeen million members.[42] Everyone working in the food sector, from the peasant farmer to those employed in food processing and the marketing of food, had to join the RNS. One single organization thus represented all areas of the food and agriculture industry. This "unified" front was quite a change from the former picture of agrarian interest organizations characterized by regional and economic differences and rivalries. The RNS was a step toward the Nazi's ideal of a corporate society where class differences no longer mattered. It was set up as a self-governing body with Darré as the head of the organization. Since he was also the Minister of Agriculture, the RNS's autonomy from the state existed only on paper.[43] Its effectiveness was also impacted by strong rivalries with other ministries and mass organizations such as the German Labor Front (*Deutsche Arbeitsfront*, or DAF). The representation of rural laborers and the question of food prices for workers were especially contentious issues and caused tensions between Darré and Robert Ley, the head of the German Labor Front.[44]

Figure 3.1. Richard Walther Darré giving a speech on December 13, 1937.
Source: **Bundesarchiv Bild 183-H1215-0503-009.**

Despite Darré's claims after the war that the RNS was independent from the Nazi Party and was in disagreement with other Nazi organizations, there is no question about its significance for the economy of the Third Reich.[45] The organization paid sixteen thousand officials and had more than seventeen thousand employees. A total of fifty thousand people worked for the organization without an honorarium.[46] It ensured complete control of the food sector and of all political activities in every village throughout Germany. It is thus hard to deny—as Darré would do after the war—the importance of the RNS and its contributions to Germany's economic preparation for war.[47]

Another important piece of agricultural legislation written by Darré and Backe was the *Erbhof* law (Law of Hereditary Entailment) designed to implement the principle of blood and soil. The law ensured that farm holdings would pass undivided to a single and racially selected heir—only "Aryans" could inherit the farm[48]—thus preserving the peasants as the "blood source of the German people," which was Darré's declared goal (*Das Bauerntum als Blutsquelle des deutschen Volkes*).[49] The oldest (or in some cases the youngest) son would become the *Erbhofbauer*—the legal heir of the entailed estate—a privileged position reserved for Germans who were physically able and had "flawless moral conduct."[50] A daughter might become the legal heir only if no suitable male family member could be found. Excluded were also those with Jewish spouses. The law came with rigorous restrictions designed to protect the farm and the "purity" of its owners. The farm could not be sold, bought, or used as security against loans. The size of the inheritance was regulated as well: the farm had to be big enough to sustain a family, and could not be larger than 125 hectares, though the maximum limit was not strictly enforced.

The *Erbhof* law was criticized for its impracticality by a variety of constituents: economists feared that the law restricted economic vitality and would impair investment in farm modernization. Business owners lamented that landed property was taken out of the market, and large landowners were threatened by the exclusion of larger estates. They feared that it represented a step toward a land reform that would break the stronghold of the rural aristocracy in the eastern parts of the country. Peasants resented the interference in inheritance decisions, the overturning of local inheritance patterns, and the built-in disadvantages for siblings and daughters. Max Sering, a leading agronomist at the time, shared Darré's interest in protecting peasant holdings, but feared that the law would ultimately hurt the peasant economy.[51] But for Darré and Backe the inheritance law had enormous symbolic value. It emphatically recognized and elevated the racially "pure" midsize peasant as the *Erbhofbauer* and was thus a crucial tool for the implementation of their agrarian ideology. It would facilitate the creation of a rural elite destined to become the new ruling class. Himmler and Hitler shared Darré's and Backe's vision and fully supported the legislation.[52]

In practice, however, the law encountered such strong hostility by peasants that its regulations had to be modified further. Special courts were established that handled individual complaints and ruled in specific cases.[53] Many exceptions were allowed and requests for special considerations granted. The implementation of the law thus gave evidence of a lot more flexibility than the initial bill had suggested. But still, farms between ten and one hundred hectares became *Erbhöfe* ("inheritance estates") and were heralded as the ideal size for a peasant family that would bring in the new era of German agriculture.[54] A massive propaganda campaign lauded peasants' patriotic service and kept any public dissatisfaction at bay. In the end, the law did not substantially alter the structure of landownership because there were not enough farms that fell into the ideal size category.

In any case, Darré and Backe treated the *Erbhof* Law as a great success. Darré acknowledged Backe's hard work and was very pleased with his protégé.[55] In a letter to his wife, Backe boasts that "our law will one day be remembered as the beginning of a new era."[56] The law remained intact until September 1943, when Backe—now as the acting Agricultural Minister—loosened some of the restrictions.[57] In his reflections after the war, Backe still considered the law one of the great achievements of Nazi agrarian politics. He predicted that "historians will look at these reforms and recognize how National Socialist policy helped to rebuild society peacefully."[58]

BACKE'S METEORIC CAREER

Backe's accomplishments did not go unnoticed. In October 1936, he was appointed Food Commissioner in Göring's Four-Year Plan administration, a job that gave him responsibilities and the power to make decisions without informing his boss in the ministry. The relationship between Darré and Backe had come to a crossroad.[59]

Initially, Backe had greatly admired Darré's skills as a politician.[60] He described Darré as "a great peasant leader; he is the only one who instinctively recognized the idea of the peasantry and held on to it."[61] In 1933, Backe still believed that Darré was "fabulous" and "very successful,"[62] and he foresaw a great political career for him.[63] This positive assessment of Darré's leadership style and abilities changed over the course of the next two years. Backe became more critical of Darré's judgment of people and did not think that he handled conflict within his department very well. The words he now used to describe Darré were quite harsh. In a letter to his wife dated July 5, 1935, Backe called Darré a "loser," "weak," and "insecure."[64] He stated that economic questions were clearly not Darré's strong suit and doubted that he was up to the task.[65] He told his wife that he was sure Darré would "fail."[66] Darré, on the other hand, valued Backe's expertise in economic questions, but had problems with his personality. He criticized Backe for his "Russian weakness in making decisions that were linked to personal vanity and an ambitious wife."[67] The two men, who had worked together on some major agricultural legislation in the early years of the Nazi regime, started distancing themselves from each other.

Darré later used these personality differences to argue that Backe had begun to strategically outmaneuver his boss. He fabricated a story that characterized himself as the harmless peasant advocate who had little to do with the racist Nazi views that led to genocide.[68] The historical record shows that Backe's and Darré's worldviews did not differ very much. Their personalities, however, clashed. Backe appears to have been much more determined, uncompromising, and dedicated to the "historic battle."[69] He considered himself to be the brain and hard worker behind the scenes, not the leader.[70] Ursula Backe shared her husband's own characterization in her diary on May 5, 1934:

> Herbert always says that it is the pride of the Backes to be like the infantry. How often did Herbert say that he wants to solve a great, difficult problem for somebody else, but that his name should not be named first. It's not that he is only following commands; instead, even then he helped Darré with his strong will and ideas, and today too, he is effective with his ideas.[71]

Between the two different personalities, Backe quickly emerged as the more effective administrator who had the expertise and got things done. It thus did not come as a surprise—except to Darré—when Göring chose Backe to be the food commissioner in the Four-Year Plan. The Four-Year Plan administration was created in 1936 to prepare Germany for war. Achieving self-sufficiency was a high priority, and the Four-Year Plan administration thus overlapped with the charges of the Ministry of Food and Agriculture. Choosing Backe, the state secretary in Darré's ministry and Darré's second man, for the post in the Four-Year Plan was a clear recognition of Backe and would inevitably lead to conflicts of authority between the two men.[72] The first such conflict was over the staffing of offices. Backe wanted to take some of the men who worked for him in the Ministry with him into the Four-Year Plan administration, but Darré felt strongly that he could not lose any of his staff. He accused his state secretary of insubordination.[73] Repeatedly over the next years, Backe felt caught between his two bosses, Darré and Göring.

It became increasingly hard to sort out the question of authority and reporting with regard to agricultural decision making. The overlapping of responsibilities was characteristic of other agencies within the Nazi regime, and it was intentional and part of the polycratic power structure. Darré became more and more defensive. He complained that Backe, as the Food Commissioner in the Four-Year Plan, was able to make decisions without consulting or at least informing Darré.[74] Darré was told that Backe's double appointment would not diminish Darré's power as minister, and that Göring would continue to turn to him for "all matters of importance."[75] But Göring did not keep his promise. In 1941, Darré tried again to put Backe in a subordinate position and demanded that responsibilities would be "clearly defined."[76] He wrote Backe a letter and "gave" him the power to make decisions in all questions regarding the war while Darré went on vacation. Darré explains that this "will show you more than any words that I personally and professionally trust you to represent me at this crucial time."[77] Darré's statement illustrates that he was out of touch with the political realities at this point in time. Darré was still the head of the Reich Food Estate, was called the Reich Peasant Leader, and held the post of the Minister of Agriculture, but his real power had vanished. Backe oversaw the complex and well-working food-rationing system and was in charge of food politics during the war. Hitler had informed Backe, not Darré, of the plans to invade the Soviet Union in early December 1940 and briefed him on the details of the military operation. Backe's expertise in food questions was more and more needed the longer the war lasted, while Darré's blood-and-soil ideology and his plans for the settlement of German peasants was less of a priority. Hitler relied on Backe's reports on the food situation and his advice on food rations and would defer to Backe for any decision with regard to food politics. Again, it was not that Darré's ideas were no longer valued—but the time was not right to implement them.

Figure 3.2. Herbert Backe, at the height of his power, June 2, 1942. *Source:* Bundesarchiv Bild 183-J02034

Backe, on the other hand, was well aware of the change in power. His response to Darré's offer to "give" him power while he was on vacation was disbelief and anger. Darré's original letter can be found in the archives. It is marked up in red pen presumably by Backe with comments such as "how dare he," "that's enough!"—a rare find of a document that gives testimony to the unedited reaction of a political figure.[78] By April 1941, Backe called Darré a "finished, a broken man," who didn't understand that "not his mission, but he himself had failed." A letter to his wife illustrates the "great contempt" he had for Darré whose downfall represented to Backe "the collapse of an egoistic man, who wanted to promote himself by any means."[79] He calls the rivalry between himself and Darré a "brotherly battle" (*Bruderkampf*) that had come to the final duel. Backe was eager to deliver the final fatal blow that would allow him to finish his job.[80]

Even though Hitler trusted Backe to make all decisions, he was hesitant to demote Darré publicly. Replacing Darré during the war could have been interpreted as indicating a problem in food policy—an impression Hitler was keen to avoid. But the dismissal of Darré was only a question of time. Without much public notice, Darré was sent on leave in May 1942, officially for medical reasons.[81] Backe took over all responsibilities as acting Reich Minister and was officially named Reich Minister of Food and Agriculture in April 1944.

When Germany turned its attention toward a war against the Soviet Union in June 1941, Backe was already the man who made the decisions with regard to food and agricultural policy. He dealt with the logistics of the food supply and would oversee the economic aspects of the invasion. The *Hungerplan* and its ruthless execution is the topic of the next chapter.

4

THE *HUNGERPLAN*

Barbarossa and the Starvation of the Soviet Union

Food and food supplies played a prominent role in the German invasion of the Soviet Union. Long before the actual attack began on June 22, 1941, Hitler had planned to invade his "ally" for economic reasons. The nonaggression pact Hitler and Stalin had signed in August 1939 was only a tactical move on Hitler's part to stall for time and prepare for the ultimate war in the East. Economic calculations and racial motivations made the war against Stalin's empire a high priority. Not only would SS *Einsatzgruppen* (mobile killing units of the SS) follow the German Army to eradicate Jews, Communists, and partisans, but the German troops were also charged with extracting agricultural surpluses and natural resources from the conquered land. After the quick defeat of the enemy, the territory in the East would be reorganized for German needs, native populations would be removed, and German farmers settled on the land. The "Greater German Reich" would become the dominant power and master of continental Europe.

To ensure the efficient exploitation of food, preparations for Operation Barbarossa had started early on. Herbert Backe had been informed of the concrete invasion plans in winter 1940. His charge was to ensure the provisioning of the invading German Army and to come up with a plan to extract the maximum resources from the conquered soil. All three million German soldiers were to be fed only on agricultural products from the

Russian soil alone. In other words, all food had to be taken from and at the expense of Soviet civilians. Backe did not want to see any "misdirected pity" for the Soviets, who were "used to hunger" and had brought this fate onto themselves. He crafted a *Hungerplan* ("hunger plan") that divided the Soviet Union into two distinct zones, the "surplus" zone consisting of the Ukraine, southern Russia, the Caucasus region, and the "deficit" zone—Belarus, northern and central Russia. People living in the deficit zone were to be sealed off from all food supplies and left to starve. Agricultural production from the fertile lands of the Ukraine and the Caucasus was to be exploited for German needs and any surplus was to be sent home.

The Nazis' carefully crafted and brutally implemented food policy thus contributed to the devastation of the Soviet Union in a way unprecedented in world history. Access to food functioned as a weapon and served German interests. During the invasion all food for the German Army came from local resources. The harvest was taken, and precious natural resources were extracted. Over two and a half years, a total of 7 million tons of grain, ¾ million tons of oil seeds, 600,000 tons of meat, and 150,000 tons of oils were taken from the Soviet Union and shipped to Germany. Another 2.3 million tons of grain were distributed to local collaborators and German civilians. In total, more than 9 million tons of grain were taken at the expense of the Soviet population. In the end, the Nazi hunger politics cost the lives of some 4 to 7 million Soviet citizens.[1]

PLANNING FOR THE "BIG THING": THE GENESIS OF THE *HUNGERPLAN*

Backe's charge was to avoid food shortages on the home front similar to those experienced during World War I at any cost. As the war went on, this became increasingly difficult to accomplish. In 1941, German food supplies had reached critically low levels and the Nazi leadership feared that with empty stomachs the support for the Nazis would dwindle quickly. The war had cut Germany off from half of its food imports, and—with England still undefeated—stalled all food imports from the Western Hemisphere. By 1941, all food reserves were exhausted. The loss of agricultural workers had taken a heavy toll on domestic production, and the shortage of chemical fertilizers, coupled with the demands of a war economy, further aggravated the situation. The sophisticated rationing system and the proposed changes in consumption to alleviate the shortages as described in earlier chapters could only do so much—and certainly did not change the basic equation of food demands and supplies. After the winter of 1941–1942, all of the six million tons of reserve in bread grains had been used up. A food shortage was imminent. To ensure food for Germans in the long term, a more radical solution was needed. The invasion of the Soviet Union served exactly that purpose. After the occupation, resources could be exploited and the agricultural economy would be restructured to serve German needs.

The agricultural resources in the Soviet Union were essential for Germany's ability to continue the war. Various trade agreements between Germany and the Soviet Union had already brought important products to Germany, and the nonaggression pact between Hitler and Stalin ensured that food deliveries continued. Hitler, however, had never intended to rely on trade agreements alone. A war against the Soviet Union had always been his plan, and he had scarcely made a secret of it. In the same month that he stunned the world with his nonaggression pact, he proclaimed that he needed "the Ukraine, in order that no one is able to starve us again like in the last war."[2] Hitler promised his military commanders that the "immense riches" of the Soviet Union would make Germany "unassailable."[3] There was no doubt that access to food and exploiting local resources was one of the main purposes of the invasion and occupation. The economic benefits of a war against the Soviet Union would not just be short-lived. The fertile lands of the Soviet Union would decrease Germany's dependency on food imports and advance the country's autarky. Ultimately, the territory would be reorganized and a new European continental market created. Goebbels confirmed again in 1942, one year into the invasion of the Soviet Union, that the war had been launched for "grain and bread, for a full breakfast, lunch and dinner table."[4]

The strategic planning for Operation Barbarossa had included economic considerations from the very beginning. On November 4, 1940, Hitler had met with his military leaders, and only a few days later Göring had shared the news of the planned invasion with the highest officials in the Four-Year Plan. Herbert Backe and his state secretaries in the Four-Year Plan administration, Paul Körner and Hans-Joachim Riecke, were charged with preparing a plan for the economic exploitation of those territories to be occupied in the future.[5] Backe and his staff met repeatedly with Hitler and Göring during the winter of 1940–1941 and prepared reports that emphasized the urgency of the food situation. In a meeting with Göring on January 13, 1941, Backe suggested the reduction of meat rations, a step that until then had not been considered because of the fear of jeopardizing support at home.[6] The only way to avoid such reductions, however, was to secure German access to the resources of the Black Earth region in the Soviet Union. The war against the Soviet Union had become an economic priority.

Among the Nazi leaders, Backe was the expert on Soviet agriculture. In the early 1920s, he had written his doctoral thesis on the Soviet agricultural system, but his dissertation committee at the University of Göttingen had not awarded him the doctorate. Backe's manuscript was republished in 1941 and distributed among Nazi officials as a rationale for the economic invasion of the Soviet Union. In the new introduction written in 1941, Backe stated that the current situation demanded the annexation of Russia into the greater European economic area. He described how Russia—or "the Russian"—had failed to use its resources and find its place in a European economy in the past. Now Germany had the chance to make things right: to use Soviet resources to feed Europe in the short run and to increase agricultural production in the long run.[7] In another publication on the European food market, Backe had argued strongly against liberalism and promoted his idea of a European continental market. The agricultural resources of Russia and parts of the USSSR were instrumental in attaining the goal of a Europe which was self-sufficient in food.[8] Land and resources in Poland and especially the Ukraine—the "granary of Europe"—were regarded as "natural" places to exploit.[9] Agricultural and economic interests were clearly at the forefront of the planning for the invasion of the Soviet Union.[10]

Backe worked feverishly on the details of the plan in spring 1941. In a letter to his wife dated April 8, 1941, he confirmed that the preparations for Operation Barbarossa were under way. He sounded upbeat and confident about the economic benefits of the invasion, a state of mind that stood in contrast to his desperation and frustration voiced in other letters. Backe emphasized the secrecy of the whole operation, but sounded excited about the possibilities and conveyed that he was planning the "big thing":

> I have thought about the measures for Barbarossa with regard to our area and have decided. Yesterday I worked until 2 a.m. on the concept. I need Göring's permission for my plan as soon as possible. Then it will be a really "big thing" [*eine ganz grosse Sache*]. In contrast to the unspeakable pressures of the last months I see everything more clearly now. The decisions are made, success is assured in my view. I just need general approval, since this is not only about agricultural problems, but about the economy as a whole.[11]

Over the next few weeks, the state secretaries under Backe's leadership crafted a plan for the economic exploitation of the Soviet Union following the invasion. On May 2, 1941, senior officials from the Reich ministries came together in Berlin to meet with General Georg Thomas, the head of the Defense Economy and Armament Office in the Wehrmacht High Command of the Armed Forces (*Wirtschafts- und Rüstungsamt im OKW.*)[12] When Riecke was questioned five years later during the Nuremberg war crime trials about his role in the planning, Backe's right-hand man had only a fuzzy memory of the sequence of the events. He stated during his interrogation: "I don't know if I participated in the meeting, but I know, that comments of this kind were made at the time. . . . I only know it from presentations or speeches made by Backe. Backe thought that logistically it would be impossible, and therefore people would have to starve there."[13] Brief summary notes from the meeting in Berlin confirmed the major decisions made by those present:

1. The war can only be continued, if the entire German Army can be fed from Russia;
2. Without doubt, tens of millions of people will die of hunger if we get what is necessary for our troops from the land; and
3. The exploitation of oilseed and oil cake has highest priority, then grains. All available fat and meat will be used by the troops.[14]

The outcome and implications of this meeting are comparable to the meeting of senior administrators at the Wannsee Conference in January 1942. In Wannsee, senior officials laid out the details for the implementation of the final solution to the Jewish question. At the May 1941 meeting, the Nazi planners agreed that millions of the Soviet population would be decimated and made a plan of how to proceed with this task.[15] The first point—to feed the German Army entirely from Soviet land—was especially important for General Thomas, who calculated that if the army's need for food and animal fodder could be met with local resources, it could use its transportation capacity to focus on fuel and ammunition. Soviet agricultural regions would provide much-needed grain and oilseeds for Germany, while Soviet urban and industrial centers would be cut off from any food supply and famine on a mass scale would occur. The protocol simply stated: "without doubt tens of millions of people will starve to death when we take what we need from the land."[16] According to Backe's calculations, the Soviet surplus population was somewhere between twenty and thirty million, exactly the number by which the urban population had grown under Stalin's industrialization campaign. Himmler used this figure again just one week before the invasion, when he stated that the forthcoming war would kill "20–30 million Slavs and Jews" by military actions and problems with food supplies.[17] Finally, Göring confirmed the count in November when he told the Italian foreign minister that twenty to thirty million Soviet citizen would starve as a consequence of the German occupation.[18]

Three weeks after the meeting of the state secretaries with General Thomas, a document was produced that confirmed the decisions from the earlier meeting. The *Economic Policy Guidelines* (*Wirtschaftspolitische Richtlinien*) from May 23 was a twenty-page document authored by the agricultural section of the Economic Staff East (*Wirtschaftsstab Ost*) under the directive of Hans-Joachim Riecke.[19] In this document, the argument is made again that Russia's food situation was desperate because of the large increase of the urban population over the last two decades. The percentage of people living in the city had risen from 10 percent of the population in 1914 to 30 percent in 1939. With its emphasis on industrialization, Russia's production of grain for export had dropped from eleven million tons on the eve of World War I to only two million tons in 1941. The *Economic Policy Guidelines* stated that Germany needed "8.7 million tons of grain from Russia, not 1 million tons."[20] The only way to extract food was by drastically reducing Soviet consumption.

To achieve this goal, the agricultural planners divided the Soviet Union into two distinct zones. Southern Russia, the Ukraine, and the Caucasus region belonged to the so-called surplus zone, while the forest area in northern and central Russia formed the "deficit" zone. Moscow, Leningrad and other industrial centers were part of the deficit zone. The deficit zone was to be sealed off. No food was to be delivered to the area and all production of food was to be stopped. All food that was saved this way would be used for German consumption and shipped to the Reich. The fate of the people living in the deficit areas was of little concern to the German planners. They would be left to fend for themselves or be moved east to Siberia. Just like the idea to ship all Jews to Madagascar, the "resettlement" of millions of Soviet citizens was logistically impossible and never a realistic option. Instead, it was calculated that millions of people would succumb to hunger and starvation. It was Backe, who had grown up in the Caucasus before World War I and had gone to Russian schools and knew Russian culture, who argued that the Soviets had brought this fate upon themselves by their inability to organize agriculture successfully. The growth of the Soviet urban population had been too fast and the country was not able to support itself. Even if the German occupiers wanted to alleviate the problems, they agreed that little could be done to prevent the death of tens of millions of people. Any attempts to save the Russian people with resources from the surplus were explicitly condemned since this would only be at the expense of Europe and of Germany's ability to continue the war. The *Guidelines* made utterly clear to everybody what would happen to the Soviet population in these territories:

> Many tens of millions of people in this territory will become superfluous and will die or must immigrate to Siberia. Attempts to rescue the population there from death through starvation by obtaining surpluses from the Black Earth zone can only be at the expense of the provisioning of Europe. They prevent the possibility of Germany holding out till the end of the war, they prevent Germany and Europe from resisting the blockade.[21]

In another document, Backe made no secret of his hatred for the Soviet people. Just one week after the circulation of the *Guidelines*, he sent a memo to the heads of the regional peasant associations (*Kreislandwirtschaftsführer*) in which he cautioned everybody not to show any "false sympathy" with "the Russian." According to Backe, "the Russian has already endured poverty, hunger and frugality for centuries." He therefore warns the peasant leaders not to "apply the German standard of living as [their] yardstick and to alter the Russian way of life."[22] In the technocratic language of the memo from June 1, 1941, Backe told the peasant leaders that "the Russian stomach is stretchable" and he sternly reminded everybody that he did not want to see any "misplaced pity."[23]

There has been some debate among historians over the authorship of this starvation policy.[24] The sources, however, leave little doubt about Backe's influence and intentions. Backe was responsible for setting food rations and he oversaw their implementation knowing full well that this would mean hunger and starvation for millions of Russians.[25] Many documents testify to Backe's desperation once the invasion had begun, but he showed little or no concern about the fate of the Jewish, Soviet, and Polish victims.[26] According to Ursula Backe, there was complete agreement among Backe, Hitler, and Alfred Rosenberg (who would become Reich Minister for the Occupied Eastern Territories) about the necessary next steps and the economic exploitation of the eastern territories. On May 30, 1941, she wrote in her diary:

> On the 14th, telephone call. Herbert to meet the *Führer* on May 15th. He gives report in the presence of Lammers, Bormann, Keitel, without Göring or Darré.[27] The *Führer* immediately asks questions about Barbarossa. Herbert reports, shows maps, reports about overall food situation. Some of it was news to the *Führer*. In general, Herbert's report just confirmed his already clear view of the situation. Also complete agreement between Rosbg. [Rosenberg] and Hbt. [Herbert] on the basics.[28]

The directives formulated in the *Richtlinien* were circulated among German officials in June as the official guidelines for the economic exploitation of the Soviet Union. One thousand copies were made of the so-called Green Folder issued on June 16.[29] The memo reiterated the provisioning of the German Army entirely off the enemy's land, and the necessity of taking the maximum amount of food and agricultural produce from Russia to be sent back home to Germany. In general "only those areas where we can find agricultural and mineral oil reserves would be supported economically."[30] In June 1941, the hunger plan (*Hungerplan*) had become official policy.

THE IMPLEMENTATION OF THE *HUNGERPLAN*

The *Hungerplan* had two main goals: to provide the German armed forces with food from the occupied lands, and to extract extra food that would be sent to Germany. Implicit in this goal was the intention of dramatically decimating the Soviet population as a way to get rid of "useless eaters."[31] This strategy would allow Germany to acquire more resources and "cleanse" the lands to make room for German settlers. The economic and strategic goals of the German invasion thus went hand in hand with the Nazis' racial ideology.

How did the German occupiers go about the actual acquisition of food supplies? The coordination of the task fell to Backe and his assistant in the Four-Year Plan, Hans-Joachim Riecke. Immediately following the invasion, an apparatus was put in place to organize the extraction and distribution of food. Following Göring's order dated July 27, 1941, the Central Trading Company East (*Zentral-Handelsgesellschaft Ost*, or *ZHO*) was formed to collect all agricultural harvest data and to ensure its redistribution according to German needs. The merchants working for the ZHO understood that the ultimate goal was "to get as much as possible from the Soviet Union."[32] Only Soviet citizens working for Germans were to be fed. Riecke even turned away requests by the military commanders who asked permission to provide for people's basic needs to avoid social unrest or resistance. The transportation of food to Germany had absolute priority over the feeding of Soviet civilians.[33]

In Belarus, for example, local agricultural production was to feed the 2.1 million soldiers of the Wehrmacht Army Group Center (*Heeresgruppe Mitte*). The directive was to be implemented swiftly and orderly, and any chaotic plundering by German soldiers had to be avoided. Local production had to continue as much as possible and precious resources could not be wasted. In reality, however, the invasion and occupation proceeded much more chaotically. Soldiers were told by their superiors to take whatever food they needed, and the troops often did so without waiting for an organized extraction plan. Plenty of sources document that soldiers of all ranks participated in the wild looting, acting as if it was their personal right to take what they needed—or what their families at home could use. Reports describe how soldiers even sent butter and other foods home to Germany.[34] Between September 1941 and August 1942, 60 percent of the grain cereals, 90 percent of the potatoes, 65 percent of the meat, and 10 percent of the fats consumed by the *Heeresgruppe Mitte* were taken from local producers in Belarus. The remaining food for this division came from the Ukraine.[35]

Over the period from July 1941 to March 1943, the German Wehrmacht took 5.6 million tons of grain from Soviet soil, and another 1.2

million tons were shipped to Germany. Grain was also distributed to collaborators. All in all, more than nine million tons of grains were taken during that time period. Compared to trade agreements before the invasion, the Soviet Union was robbed of more than twice that amount of grain for German consumption.[36] Germans also took meat, oil, potatoes, and other foods—all at the expense of the Soviet people. After an inspection of the Ukraine, Riecke described the situation on January 26, 1942, as follows: "Behind the front is an area of approximately 150 km that is completely stripped bare ('*Kahlfrass*')."[37]

Backe's plan also included a radical restructuring of Soviet agriculture under German supervision. Under Stalin, the Soviet peasant had become a worker on a collective farm, or *kolkhoz*. The German occupiers now wanted to give Soviet peasants greater autonomy and provide incentives for increased production. But even if this kind of restructuring would have been successful, the economic planners knew that little if any surplus was actually available and that the acquisition of food meant taking whatever was needed to survive from the Soviets. Among the foremost victims of Nazi food policy were people in the cities. The *Hungerplan* had slated large urban centers such as Leningrad to be sealed off from all supplies and the population devastated by starvation. Hitler had made clear that sealing areas off rather than accepting capitulation and occupation was more desirable, precisely because of food. The city of Leningrad endured this trauma for almost three years, from fall 1941 to early 1944. German troops surrounded the city in October 1941, trapping 2.5 million civilians and soldiers. Already by December, inhabitants faced severe hunger. People died at a rate of almost four thousand a day. Over the next eleven months, 653,000 Leningraders would die of hunger.[38] Over the course of the occupation, an estimated one million people perished from starvation and related causes in Leningrad alone. One such victim was an eleven-year-old girl named Tania Savicheva. Tania kept a diary in which she noted the deaths of her family and friends between December 1941 and May 1942. Her last entry in 1942 reads: "Everybody died. Only Tania is left." Tania died in 1944.[39]

Hitler's plans for the city of Leningrad—its siege and the misery of its 3.5 million inhabitants—are relatively well known even though they are rarely contextualized within the greater framework of the Nazis' genocidal food policy. But other Soviet cities fared no better: fifty thousand people died in the capital of Ukraine, Kiev, during the German occupation.[40] Another twenty thousand people died in the city of Charkow. Historians estimate that roughly half of the Soviet population experienced serious hunger under the German occupation.[41] Only those people the Germans could use as workers were to be given any food; others were deliberately left to die. Food rations for those who worked for Germany were slightly higher, but they were hardly enough to survive the back-breaking labor in German mines or ammunition factories. The death rate among those forced laborers was just as high as in the camps.[42]

In 1942, the principles of the *Hungerplan*—the sealing off and starvation of Soviet cities as well as the exploitation and reorganization of Soviet agriculture—were extended to other occupied eastern territories. Food shortages in Germany had reached critical levels and ration cuts seemed unavoidable. For Göring, the paradox of controlling large parts of Europe but yet not having enough food for Germans was unacceptable. On August 6, 1942, he fumed that "I have to give a bread ration to the German people which can no longer be justified. I have had foreign workers, regardless of where they come from, declare that they had better food at home than here in Germany. . . . The *Führer* repeatedly said, and I repeat his words: if any one has to go hungry, it shall not be the Germans, but other people. In every one of the occupied territories, I see the people being fed abundantly and among our own people there is starvation."[43]

Only a radical step could change the situation. The occupied area of Poland, the so-called *Generalgovernment*, or General Government, which was under colonial administration of Germany and had been used as a labor reservoir as well as a "dumping ground" for those the Nazis considered inferior, was now to become subject to starvation policies as well. Until then, the economic needs of the German Reich for foreign workers had allowed for small food rations to be distributed. From now on, however, all food deliveries from Germany to Poland were to stop, and here as well, the German Army had to be fed from local resources alone. Jews in the ghettos and camps were excluded from all food supplies, and surpluses had to be extracted and shipped to Germany.

The extension of the *Hungerplan* to other areas came just after a change in leadership at the highest level. In April 1942, the Minister of Food and Agriculture, Richard Walther Darré had been sent on leave and was replaced by Backe as the acting minister. Hitler had long been convinced that Backe was the right man and better equipped to prevent a food crisis. He had already turned to Backe for any major decision, as a diary entry from Ursula Backe in July 1941 illustrates. She wrote here about her husband briefing Hitler on food issues in the occupied territories. After the briefing, she quotes Hitler as saying: "What's Backe's opinion? What did Backe say? What does Backe say?"[44] Food shortages continued in Germany throughout the year and took on more critical levels in spring 1942. When further ration cuts seemed unavoidable, Hitler decided that he could no longer wait and replaced Darré. Backe was now fully in charge of food policy and worked diligently to implement the vision of Himmler, Göring, and Hitler.

This decision to extend the *Hungerplan* to other occupied eastern territories shows how closely food policy and the Holocaust were connected. In 1942, the mass murder of Jews accelerated dramatically. Responding to the protest of administrators that they could not cut Polish rations any further, Backe stated: "In the Generalgovernment there are currently still 3.5 million Jews. Poland is to be sanitized within the coming year."[45] The directive was implemented quickly and efficiently. All food was to be extracted from the General Government, and the death camps in Treblinka, Chelmno, and Belzec were made fully operational. By the end of 1942, very few Polish Jews were still alive. At the same time, a good fall harvest in the General Government had greatly increased food deliveries to Germany and secured food rations. In 1942–1943, more than half of the rye and potato imports and 66 percent of oat imports came from the General Government.[46] The *Hungerplan* had worked. Rations in Germany were not cut any further while millions of "useless eaters" in Poland and the Soviet Union were killed. The Nazi hunger policy had expedited the final solution.

SOVIET POWS

The connection between Nazi food policy and genocide also becomes evident in the case of Soviet POWs. Soviet POWs were the largest group of victims targeted by the *Hungerplan*. The German Army took hundreds of thousands of Soviet soldiers prisoner in the first weeks of the invasion. Six months into the Barbarossa campaign the number had reached more than 3.3 million.[47] Two million of these prisoners had died by spring 1942. About six hundred thousand were shot, but most of them had succumbed to starvation and maltreatment.[48] Of the 5.7 million Soviet soldiers captured between 1941 and 1945, a total of 3.3 million died.[49]

The murderous treatment of captured Soviet soldiers was not the unexpected outcome of a grandiose invasion that lasted longer and was more difficult to win than had been anticipated by the military planners. Nor was it the sheer number of prisoners that made feeding and housing them impossible. The comparison with the Western front shows that there, too, millions had been taken prisoner by the Germans, but their death rate was much lower. On the Western front, less than 5 percent of the captured soldiers died in German hands, compared to a death rate of 57.5 percent over the course of the war among Red Army soldiers in German captivity.[50] The mass dying of Soviet captured soldiers was due to a genocidal food policy fueled by racism and disdain for the "inferior" Slavs—after June 1941, Soviet soldiers also were at the bottom of the racial hierarchy and were treated accordingly. In the Nazi mind, the multiethnic Soviets were all "Russians." They were politically dangerous and racially inferior. In German captivity, they all became "useless mouths" to be fed—something that the Nazis did not want to see done at the expense of the German population.[51]

From the beginning, the war in the East was considered a war of annihilation with no regard for the lives of the enemy. The planning for Operation Barbarossa had always included taking a large number of POWs, but no preparations had been made in advance to provide shelter and food for the captured soldiers. Their death was thus clearly part of the plan.[52] Military orders called for ruthless treatment and swift killing of Soviet soldiers. On June 6, 1941, a Commissar Order was issued demanding that any Soviet political commissar among the captured troops would be shot, as well as any prisoner suspected to be a political leader. Following this directive, more than half a million captured Soviet soldiers—including all Jewish soldiers—were selected by the German troops and turned over to the SS to be executed. Soviet soldiers who surrendered or were wounded were shot as well. International laws on the treatment of enemy soldiers and prisoners such as the 1929 Geneva Convention or the 1907 Hague Convention were deliberately ignored, and soldiers had explicit orders to treat the enemy with toughness and an uncompromising attitude. The "Guidelines for the Conduct of the Army in Russia" from May 1941 demanded "ruthless and energetic measures against Bolshevik rabble-rousers . . . and the total elimination of any active and passive resistance." Supplemental instructions issued in July ordered German soldiers to treat prisoners of war in ways "that bear in mind the fierceness and the inhuman brutality of the Russian during battle."[53] A German soldier who showed any leniency toward the "Russian" or who treated him as a human being would be punished severely.[54] With the official sanctioning and even expectation of the killing of Soviet captured soldiers, the brutality of the German troops knew few limits. In fact, the highest military leadership explicitly condoned the brutal treatment of Soviet soldiers.

Since no permanent shelters or camps had been built in advance to house the captured soldiers, the prisoners were kept in temporary and transit camps behind the front. Hundreds of thousands of them were marched to camps at great distances and many of the malnourished and weakened prisoners died during these marches to remote collection sites. Since food was reserved for German soldiers or shipped away, Soviet soldiers' rations were well below the minimum necessary to survive.[55] The first six months of the invasion proved the deadliest for Soviet POWs. An average of six thousand POWs died per day.[56] By early December 1941, 1.4 million POWs were dead. The month of November saw the highest number of deaths when weakened bodies succumbed to starvation by the hundreds of thousands. Insufficient food was the main reason for the mass deaths of captured Soviet soldiers, but insufficient shelter and brutal transportation to the camps increased the death toll.

Following the directive of the starvation policy, Soviet POWs were to receive only a minimum of the "most primitive food."[57] They were at the bottom of the food hierarchy and their basic survival needs were purposefully ignored. In the beginning, no specific rations were set at all for the prisoners, only general orders to use as little food as possible. Daily meals often did not exceed seven hundred calories, and death followed within weeks. Even when official rations were set in August 1941 at 1,490 calories per day, there was little intention to enforce the actual amount.[58] Official rations were drastically lowered in October when mass starvation among Soviet POWs was already well under way. Prisoners were not to receive any meat at all, fats were lowered by more than a third, and potatoes were replaced with turnips. Everybody was reminded again that any extra food given to a Soviet soldier "would have to be taken away from relatives at home or from German soldiers."[59] Göring confirmed the food hierarchy that governed food distribution:

> First there are the combat troops, then the other troops in enemy territory, and then the home troops. Rations have to be adjusted accordingly. After that the German civilian population will be fed. Only after that comes the civilian population in the occupied territories. In general, only those working for us in the occupied territories should receive food rations. Even if one wanted to feed all other inhabitants, one could not do so in the newly occupied eastern territories.[60]

The quote is remarkable in two ways. Göring clearly stated that it was never the intention to feed Soviet civilians, and POWs were not even mentioned as a group that needed to be fed. Even if there was extra food that could not be shipped to Germany, it was to be saved and kept as a reserve rather than distributed to Soviet prisoners.

By the end of 1941, a different economic emergency caused the questioning of the deadly food policy. The German Reich needed more people to work in agriculture and industry to replace German men who had been drafted or lost. Economic planners argued that rations for prisoners who were able to work should be increased so that they were strong enough for the hard labor. Studies were done to determine the minimum amount of food necessary for the body to keep working without "wasting" precious food resources.[61] In November, rations for selected prisoners were increased and their housing improved. Some even received basic medical support. Still, Göring reminded everyone that "the Russian can be fed easily and without interference to the German food balance. He should not be spoiled or get used to German food."[62] Food rations should only be slightly higher than for Russians at home, where "people lived in caves (*Erdhöhlen*)."[63] Some prisoners were sent to work in the countryside in Germany where food supplies were better. After regaining some strength they were assigned jobs as laborers in the armament industry. The horrendous working conditions in the mines and factories led to the death of many of these slave laborers.[64] Overall, even the need for workers on German farms and industry did not increase rations sufficient for survival. The mass deaths of captured Soviet soldiers continued.

In addition to hunger rations, the brutal movement of POWs to far distant prisoner camps caused death on a large scale. Again, the comparison with the Western front suggests that it was not the logistics that led to the countless losses of life. In the West, 1.9 million prisoners were transported to camps by trains and army trucks. On the Eastern front, army leaders insisted on marching soldiers to the far distant camps since army equipment could not be spared. To reach the camps in East Prussia and those in German-occupied Poland, prisoners had to cover twenty-five to forty kilometers per day for several weeks. After the battle of Kiev, prisoners were marched up to four hundred kilometers to camps in the Ukraine.[65] Those who could not continue walking were treated brutally, often shot on the spot, and left for dead on the streets. When temperatures turned freezing during the winter months, the marches became unfeasible and trains had to be used for the transportation of the prisoners.

Those soldiers who survived the brutal conditions of the march faced conditions impossible to survive in the camps. No preparation or planning had gone into how to actually house the masses of prisoners. They were kept in transit or permanent camps without registering their names—another violation of international law and a required practice even in the concentration camps. No record was to be kept of the calculated mass killing of captured Soviet soldiers.[66] Prisoners were held unsheltered from the elements, packed together behind barbed wire without a place to sit down or to relieve themselves. They dug holes in the earth, or built primitive barracks with grass and pieces of wood. They did not receive any food or drinks for days. When meager bread rations arrived, chaos and fighting started. Prisoners turned to grass, bark, or anything else that could be found and even instances of cannibalism occurred. Stories of the bestial behavior of the Russian soldiers were used to fuel the racial hatred. When a fire broke out in a camp in Belarus, thousands of prisoners burned to death. Others were shot while trying to escape from the burning site. Camp guards were instructed to use their weapons and were punished if they did not comply. During the winter of 1941–1942, many prisoners froze to death in the camps, since no provisions had been made to protect them from the temperatures that were often below freezing.

Insufficient shelter, the brutal conditions of the death marches and most importantly, the insufficient food led to the mass death of Soviet POWs. The high death rate was not the outcome of an emergency situation or a war gone wrong. It was the anticipated result, and part of the *Hungerplan*, that calculated that millions of Russians had to die for Germans to live and win the war.

Overall, the ambitious goal of the *Hungerplan*—to kill tens of millions of Soviets by starvation—could not be fully implemented. Instead of the envisioned "tens of millions of people," "only" four to seven million Soviet citizens died as a consequence of the murderous food policy. Systematic starvation turned out to be harder than originally thought, or as one economic historian has put it, "it is much easier to conquer territory than to redistribute calories."[67] The failure of the *Blitzkrieg* Operation Barbarossa and the lack of planning for a longer war stalled the full implementation of the *Hungerplan*. There was simply not enough manpower to seal off the "deficit areas" from their agricultural surroundings or to locate, extract, and transport any "surplus" food. With the heavy fighting that continued all around, the Wehrmacht could not spare any men to isolate cities and cut off roads. German soldiers were more concerned with acquiring food for themselves than making sure that no Russians received any food. Since local food supplies were often not enough to feed the invading army, it had to be brought in from other places as well. Finally, the plan had not accounted for the ability of people in the cities to resist and to circumvent the siege. Some found ways to get out of the city; others succeeded in locating food in the countryside. They bartered on the black market and were somehow able to hang on to life.

Even if the actual number of victims was smaller than envisioned, the food policy was still a murderous tool. Food was drastically redistributed, and millions of others starved so that Germans had enough to eat. For the majority of Soviet soldiers in German captivity, for Jews who were forced into ghettos and transported to concentration camps, and for hundreds of thousands of civilians in the cities, hunger and death by starvation was the horrific reality. Nothing was done to stop the dying or improve food rations. The mass murder was a crucial part of the *Hungerplan*, and its goals were largely accomplished.[68]

5

THE SCIENCE OF FOOD

SCIENTIFIC RESEARCH UNDER THE NAZIS

Considering the prominent role food played for the Nazis' ideology, it is not surprising that Hitler's regime heavily utilized the sciences as a tool in its quest for greater food autarky and German expansion in the East. The field of agricultural sciences was of special importance for the Nazi regime. Experimentation with food production, studies on the connection between food intake and labor productivity, and research on plant and animal breeding all promised to solve some of the greatest shortcomings of the German economy during the war.[1]

By the 1930s, Germany had established a strong tradition of scientific research. German scientists were internationally recognized leaders in their fields and they actively experimented in laboratories, universities, and research institutes. Germany's most prestigious research institution was the Kaiser Wilhelm Society (*Kaiser-Wilhelm-Gesellschaft*, or KWS). It had been founded in 1911 to promote research in the natural sciences and served as an umbrella organization for numerous research institutes. The scientists working for the Kaiser Wilhelm institutes were exempt from teaching at their universities and devoted themselves to their studies and received often generous state funding. After the Nazis came to power, the various Kaiser Wilhelm institutes continued their work, albeit cleansed of Jewish researchers and with closer supervision by the state.[2] The Nazi regime greatly supported the sciences and utilized them for their own goals. Food autarky, racial hygiene, and ultimately the war effort itself all benefited from experimentation and advancements in the sciences, and many of the institutes expanded their work during the Third Reich. New research centers were erected also in the occupied territories, where German scientists encountered new opportunities and often benefited from the know-how and work already done by other researchers.[3]

The findings of agricultural researchers contributed to the war effort in important ways. Biologists were busy adapting new plants from distant places to German soil and climate conditions. They experimented with plants that provided the war-essential rubber, and they used POWs for free labor or as "guinea pigs" in their research projects.[4] In the wake of the occupation of other countries, German scientists had access to sensitive data and were bound only by their own ethical standards. One study, for example, included a great number of prisoners and aimed at maximizing labor output with minimal food resources, while other scientists devoted energy to growing specialized produce on farms near concentration camps.[5]

While the scientists understood themselves and their work as independent and objective, there was often a great overlap between their scientific research and Nazi ideology. Many collaborated with the regime in return for increased funding and continuing support.[6] For example, biological researchers at the Kaiser Wilhelm institutes worked closely with the medical laboratory in the concentration camp in Auschwitz-Birkenau on finding a scientific method for determining race.[7] Scientists went on expeditions to the occupied territories and plundered Russian research laboratories. They brought home native plants and local collections that could be useful for their own research, and many scientists had no qualms about appropriating resources and profiting from war and occupation.[8]

The Nazi State pumped large amounts of money into this kind of research. The Kaiser Wilhelm Institute for Plant Breeding Research (*KWI für Züchtungsforschung*), for example, received 80 percent of its budget in 1943 from the Ministry of Food and Agriculture.[9] In return, the Nazi regime closely monitored the research conducted at the institute. A new umbrella organization, the Reich Research Council (*Reichsforschungsrat*, RFR), reviewed research proposals, screened researchers, and made decisions about the distribution of funding.[10] Projects that supported the war effort were generously sponsored. The Reich Minister of Food and Agriculture himself sat on the Reich Research Council, and in July 1941 Backe became its first vice president.[11]

The research conducted at the KWI for Plant Breeding Research in Müncheberg and the Institute for Animal Breeding in Dummerstorf (*KWI für Tierzuchtforschung*) was particularly close to Backe's heart. At the institute in Dummersdorf near Rostock, scientists examined the effect of fodder crops on milk production and animal breeding, research that promised to remedy the deficit in animal fat experienced in Germany. Backe had promoted the formation of the new institute, and it was no coincidence that Darré's former professor and mentor, Gustav Fröhlich, became the first director of the institute in 1938.[12] At the KWI for Plant Breeding in Müncheberg near Berlin scientists experimented with plants that had a high content in oil and protein such as soy beans, sunflowers, and rape. Others sought to increase the production of fodder crops such as clover and alfalfa, all crucial for increasing Germany's self-sufficiency.

With the invasion of the Soviet Union in 1941, new opportunities opened up for the German researchers. Russian scientists had conducted some groundbreaking research in genetics, for example, and Germans used these findings to enhance their own understanding and continued the research. They undertook field trips and excursions into the occupied lands and took plants, equipment, and data.[13] The Reich Research Council sponsored these botanical expeditions and the trips were escorted by the military to ensure safety for the traveling scientists.[14] The German scientists' vision to create a large network of research institutes and laboratories that stretched from the "Polar Sea to the Mediterranean, from the Atlantic to the extreme Continental region, from the ocean to the Alps" was well in line with the Nazis' grandiose plans to re-create a greater continental German Reich, where other populations would serve German masters.[15] To strengthen Germany's presence in the East, three new institutes for agricultural research were founded.[16] Backe was especially fond of the creation of the Institute for Agricultural Work Studies (*KWI für landwirtschaftliche Arbeitswissenschaft*) in Breslau in December 1940. He sat on the board of trustees and carefully monitored its work on the rationalization and industrialization of agricultural work, on rural emigration, and other questions of work productivity.[17]

The scientists were aware of the connection between politics and their own research. Some even considered their work to be a kind of "foreign policy" since their research enhanced Germany's international reputation.[18] The "political" mission of the Institute for Plant Breeding Research, according to one scientist, was to "create or improve useful plants that will allow for a denser settlement of the whole Northeast and Eastern territory as well as other border regions."[19]

Several Nazi organizations worked closely with the research institutes to gain insight into areas of importance to them. The Four-Year-Plan administration, the Reich Food Estate, the SS, and the German Army all funded specific research projects that promised to solve deficiencies in cotton and linen, or they pumped money into the cultivation of plants like the *kok-saghyz*.[20] Kok-saghyz, also called rubber root or Russian dandelion, was a plant that grew in a moderate climate. Soviet researchers had recently discovered that rubber (*Kautschuk*), could be derived from the plant. The German chemical company IG Farben produced a synthetic *Kautschuk* that could be mixed with the plant product to make a stronger rubber. Because of the great need for rubber during the war—for the tires of military vehicles, for example—the research with natural *Kautschuk* had great strategic value for the Nazis and was extensively supported.[21]

The close collaboration between the research institutes and the Nazi state demonstrates how important the science of food was for the Nazi regime and for the war. Heinrich Kraut's experiment with Russian prisoners of war and Joachim Caesar's plant breeding station in a satellite camp of Auschwitz can serve as examples of how easily German scientists accepted the brutal realities of the Nazi State and prioritized their scientific discoveries over moral principles.

FOOD AND LABOR PRODUCTIVITY: THE "OPERATION CABBAGE"

One research project that was funded by Herbert Backe's Ministry of Food and Agriculture was a study that looked into the correlation between food intake and labor productivity. The project was led by Heinrich Kraut, a chemist and leading scientist at the KWI for Labor Physiology (*KWI für Arbeitsphysiologie*) in Dortmund.[22] Kraut also served as the advisor to the Ministry of Food. Kraut's study involved thousands of Russian POWs and a small number of Italian prisoners who worked in the coal mines in the Ruhr area. Research that aimed at increasing labor productivity had high priority because of the dramatic shortage of laborers in Germany. Most men had been drafted to the front and major industries lacked workers. In coal mining, for example, productivity was down more than 25 percent in 1943, and severe shortages in coal led to the introduction of coal rationing in 1944. Coal production could not be increased without a great number of foreign workers. Because of the economic pressure, Hitler had allowed the increased employment of Soviet POWs in October 1941, and by December 1943 almost half of the coal miners in the Ruhr were from other countries, with Soviet nationals making up 75 percent of the foreigners.[23] Their labor productivity, however, was so low—Russian POWs produced only half the amount of other workers—that their employment did not make up for the deficit. In the eyes of some Nazi officials, the low labor output did not even justify the meager rations that were given to the prisoners. Nazi officials charged scientists to examine ways to raise the prisoners' productivity and gave clear instructions not to spend too many resources on Russian laborers.

The main reasons for the low productivity of Russian prisoners in German industry were the horrific working and living conditions. Many of the prisoners arrived in Germany wounded or sick and were half-starved and their bodies weakened from their ordeal. They were used for the hardest physical labor, working in coal mines deep underground, and often enduring brutal mistreatment by German overseers. Upon arrival in Germany, some of them were first sent to the countryside where food conditions were somewhat better, but as soon as they had regained some strength they were moved to industrial areas to work in the mines.[24] The prisoners were housed in crowded barracks, with no electricity or running water. When allied bombing of cities and urban areas increased, the prisoners were not allowed to seek shelter in bunkers and many of them died in the raids.[25] The food they received was barely enough to survive and their bodies deteriorated quickly. While Soviet POWs selected for work in the Third Reich overall fared slightly better compared with their comrades in prison camps behind the front, the death rates among these workers were also extremely high.[26]

Here is where the sciences came in. The main goal of the proposed scientific study, the so-called *Krautaktion* ("Operation Cabbage," which was a play on the last name of the scientist "Kraut," literally translated as "cabbage")[27] was to come up with a precise formula of how many additional calories were needed to extract the maximum amount of labor. Once labor productivity increased, the new amount of calories was to be distributed to more prisoners. Food distribution was to be monitored closely, since any increase in the body weight of the workers was considered unnecessary. If the body weight of the worker continued to increase even after labor productivity was maximized, food rations were to be adjusted downward. In this study, like in many others, the Nazis clearly used the sciences to serve their racist worldview and economic goals. Among the scientists, there was little or no concern about the horrific conditions experienced by their research subjects. The researchers knew about the circumstances under which their subjects were held, but the scientists did not mention these conditions in their reports. Neither did they question the validity of their data or the ethics of their study. Scientists like Kraut continued to use forced laborers as subjects for their research. The scientists may not have contributed directly to the suffering of the prisoners, but by ignoring their horrendous living conditions, their scientific work ultimately contributed to and stabilized the murderous regime.

Kraut's large study was based on an earlier, much smaller experiment he had conducted with coal miners in the Ruhr.[28] In late 1943 and early 1944, Kraut had measured the labor productivity of a small number of Russian forced laborers and examined how productivity increased when food rations were augmented by additional calories. The hypothesis was simple. Food provided the body with energy that could be used for physical labor. Fewer calories meant less energy and thus less work. More food gave the body more energy that translated into more physical labor. The results of Kraut's first study confirmed this assumption. The productivity of the Russian workers increased according to the supplements in calories. The effect of increased calories on labor productivity was immediate—already after four weeks, the Russian workers filled more wagons of coal per day than they had with smaller rations. Kraut continued the study to fine-tune the results and to come up with the exact minimum amount of food that was needed to increase productivity and stabilize body weight. Again, the scientist's goal was optimum efficiency, without "wasting" food on the Russians. Even if Kraut concluded at the end of his study that nutrition levels for the workers needed to be increased to achieve greater labor productivity, his recommendation did not come out of concern for the well-being of the workers (they still received fewer calories than the German coal workers), but because of the interest in optimal exploitation of labor productivity.[29]

This first small yet conclusive study was instrumental in convincing Reich Minister Backe to support the much larger research project proposed by Kraut. On May 23, 1944, Kraut met with Backe, a few other regional Nazi officials and Albert Voegeler, the director of *Vereinigte Stahlwerke*, a large steel and coal concern and president of the Kaiser Wilhelm Society from 1941 to 1945 to discuss the plan.[30] Voegeler was interested in the study to increase labor activity and hoped to get the full support of the Reich Ministry. He described the dismal situation among workers, and the loss of many workers due to sickness and death. Kraut's plan was to include more than ten thousand workers in the study and thus significantly impact labor productivity in the participating coal and steel mines. Backe gave the green light, and Kraut and his team made preliminary visits to the selected coal and steel mines. In the end, more than six thousand workers participated in the study. About two-thirds of them were Soviet POWs; the rest were Italian workers and a few laborers from Eastern Europe.[31]

As in his first study, Kraut demonstrated that labor productivity was closely linked to food intake. Again, other factors such as labor and living conditions were not factored into the experiment. The directives given by Kraut and his team to the participating workers also showed the racist and brutal dimension of the research. The prisoners were informed before the study began that the extra calories would be taken away if labor productivity did not increase after four to six weeks. Also, as mentioned, if any of the starved workers reached an average body weight, their calories would be adjusted accordingly. Hunger and the fear of receiving less food drove many of the workers to work as hard as possible, and often led to the exhaustion of the bodies even before the increased rations arrived. This alone should have raised questions about the usefulness of the scientific results of the study. It did not, which demonstrated the ruthlessness of the scientists and the moral choices they made. Furthermore, the scientists knew that it was not the amount of calories alone, but also the nutritional value of the increased rations that mattered for the output. There was little oversight of the actual increased ration, and random checkups showed that the extra food often did not even reach the worker.[32]

None of these problems caused Kraut to discontinue his research or to question his data. He proceeded with the study until the end of December 1944. Preliminary reports confirmed that the labor productivity of the workers increased with extra food rations. Kraut did not get to write the final report in spring 1945, because American troops entered the Ruhr region and occupied the Institute on April 13, 1945. His sponsor, Voegler, committed suicide, while Kraut and the other scientists used the results of the study to kindle their careers after the war.[33]

PLANT BREEDING IN AUSCHWITZ

Many other experiments with food were carried out under the umbrella of scientific research. One such research project that was watched closely by Heinrich Himmler involved prisoners from the concentration camp in Auschwitz. The fertile soil in the area surrounding the camp and the availability of free labor convinced Himmler that Auschwitz would be a perfect place to build plant breeding stations, to grow produce, and to conduct agricultural research. In November 1940, the commandant of the concentration camp, Rudolf Höss, met with Himmler and gave him a report on the possibilities of agricultural developments in the area. Himmler was immediately on board and instructed Höss to turn Auschwitz into "*the* agricultural research station for the eastern territories."[34] The possibilities seemed to have no limits. With an endless supply of laborers from the camps, all necessary agricultural experiments were to be conducted in Auschwitz. Big laboratories and nurseries were to be erected and stations for animal breeding built. The village of Rajsko, located only three kilometers away from the main concentration camp, was selected for the project. In the winter of 1940–1941, the small village was emptied of its Polish inhabitants and settled with SS families.

On March 1, 1941, Himmler visited Rajsko and ordered that the work start immediately. Prisoners from Auschwitz were ordered to prepare the soil and create vegetable and flower gardens. Rye was cultivated on the meadows of the former village. Laboratories, greenhouses, and nurseries were set up in existing or newly erected buildings. In July 1943, barracks were built to house the prisoners permanently instead of having them walk to work from the main camp in Auschwitz. This subordinate camp in Rajsko was put under the leadership of Joachim Caesar, an *SS Obersturmbannführer* who had a doctorate in agricultural science and botany from the University of Halle. Rajsko's most important research focused on the rubber plant kok-saghyz. Scientists experimented with a variety of the Asian plant that contained a higher percentage of rubber in its botanical makeup, and tried to acclimate the plant to the soil and weather conditions of Western Europe. The seeds of the original kok-saghyz plant came from Poland.[35]

To conduct the research, Caesar employed inmates with scientific expertise—engineers, chemists, and biologists—from Auschwitz and other concentration camps such as the women's camp in Ravensbrück. Rajsko's *Kommando Pflanzenzucht* (Brigade Plant Breeding) alone employed 150 women.[36] The living conditions in the satellite camp in Rajsko were better compared to the main camp in Auschwitz. According to some accounts, Caesar treated the female prisoners well. They received better clothing and more food than the inmates in other camps. The labor, however, was still hard, and punishment and mistreatment occurred. German SS overseers intimidated the prisoners and threatened them with a transfer back to Auschwitz, where their chances to survive were small. This way, the SS exploited the prisoners and could extract as much labor as possible.[37]

Just like Kraut's Operation Cabbage, the plant and breeding stations in the lager in Rajsko serve as an example of the selfish behavior of scientists who furthered their personal ambitions and their own research agendas. They disregarded the inhumane circumstances of their studies and thus ultimately contributed to and benefitted from a murderous regime. Scientific curiosity overruled any hesitations the scientists might have had with regard to using prisoners for their research. Most of them paid little attention to the circumstances under which the experiments were conducted.[38] The use of prison laborers for their scientific work is just one example of this shameless exploitation. Even if some of the scientists can be credited with treating the prisoners well, they still participated in the brutal experiments and were masters over life and death of the workers.

The scientists' work during the Nazi era did not negatively impact their careers after the war. Heinrich Kraut, for example, used some of the findings from his research during the war for his publications after 1945 and he quickly pursued a successful career as a food scientist.[39] Kraut became the president of the *Deutsche Gesellschaft für Ernährung* (German Nutrition Society) in 1956. In 1963, he received the *Bundesverdienstkreuz* (Federal Cross of Merit of the Federal Republic of Germany) and an honorary doctorate from the University of Münster, two of the highest honors bestowed upon a scientist in Germany. He lived for another thirty years after that until he died in 1992 at the age of ninety-eight.

GREEN NAZIS?

The Nazis' emphasis on food and agriculture, as well as their interest in nature and conservation, has brought up repeatedly the connotation of the Nazis as "green," as early supporters of nature conservation and as environmentalists.[40] The Nazis idealized nature and used it repeatedly in their propaganda as a metaphor for German cultural values and "racial characteristics." Some high-ranking Nazi officials publicly promoted organic farming, used herbal medicine, and depicted themselves as nature lovers or friends of animals. Hitler's self-declared vegetarianism was employed in propaganda as was his love of animals—especially the affection for his German shepherd—and they are still mentioned in biographies and popular accounts today. Other Nazi leaders like Göring or Himmler are also often described as animal lovers. Göring himself was an adamant hunter and was adorned with a new title as the *Reichsjägermeister* ("Reich Chief Huntmaster"). His office, the Reich Forest Service (*Reichsforstamt*), was given authority over conservation issues.[41] In his speech to SS leaders in October 1943 in which he openly talked about the ongoing extermination of Jews, Himmler went so far to claim that Germany was "the only nation of the world with a decent attitude toward animals."[42]

Under Göring's leadership, the Nazi regime introduced legislation that supported species protection and animal rights. The regulations culminated in the National Conservation Law (*Reichsnaturschutzgesetz*) of 1935. Already in November 1933, the Nazis had passed the Reich Animal Protection Law (*Reichstierschutzgesetz*) that restricted hunting and regulated the slaughter of animals. A ban on vivisection forbade experiments with animals (even though the ban had to be lifted and numerous exceptions were allowed because of protests from leading scientists), and harsh punishments were introduced for the torture and inhumane treatment of man's fellow creatures. Hitler's personal affection for animals also became apparent in his 1940 veto of a proposal from the food administration that would have limited the number of pets per family. The regulation had intended to reserve scarce food reserves for humans, but limiting the number of a family's animal companions seemed to go too far. In the end, the regulation was applied only to Jewish households while all others were allowed to keep their pets.

Nazi Germany was one of the first countries to enact a comprehensive Nature Conservation Law (*Reichsnaturschutzgesetz*) that called for the

Figure 5.1. Adolf Hitler and Eva Braun with dogs, June 14, 1942. Source: Bundesarchiv B 145 Bild-F051673-0059.

conservation of Germany's flora and fauna. The 1935 law went further than any nature conservation legislation at the time.[43] It actively promoted landscape protection and restricted developments that would "deface" or harm nature in any way. The law also allowed for the expropriation of ecologically or culturally important land from private owners and it initiated the creation of Germany's first nature reserves. All government agencies were required to consult with conservationists before any building projects could be approved. During the planning and construction of the *Autobahn*, for example, engineers had to work closely with conservationists to ensure that the landscape was protected and nature preserved.[44] The emphasis on the appearance of the countryside and its conservation was revolutionary at the time. Several nature conservation and animal protection laws practiced in Germany today derive from legislation first enacted during the Third Reich.

The forest was a part of nature that was especially close to the Germans' hearts. New laws introduced by the Nazis protected the ecosystem and health of the German forest. The legislation mandated the cultivation of a variety of trees and aimed at creating a habitat for diverse animals and plants. The Nazis introduced the *Dauerwald* ("eternal forest") concept that changed commonly used clear-cutting techniques. Until then, it had been the practice to cut trees that were of similar age and height at the same time. The idea of the eternal forest, in contrast, called for the continuous cutting of trees that were different in age and species. This new concept reversed the trend of monoculture and was designed to create a healthy ecosystem with a variety of plants and animals.[45]

The German *Wald* (forest) had great symbolic value for German culture. It had long been cherished in folk tradition, literature, and the arts, and the Nazis made its protection a high priority. The symbolism of the eternal forest was in line with the Nazi vision of a German Reich that would last an eternity, or at least "a thousand years" (Hitler often spoke of the Thousand-Year Reich that he wanted to create).[46] Like in many other areas, however, Nazi ideology differed significantly from practice, and the forest was no exception. By the mid-1930s, the great demand for wood, rather than ecological or mythical considerations, dictated forest policy. Once the war had started, the protection of the forest could not be assured. German forests were cut down faster than ever before, and deforestation also occurred in the occupied territories without any regard for the ecosystem.[47]

Landscape planning was another area where the Nazi regime took into consideration the advice of the conservation movement. *Autobahn* planners needed the approval of nature conservationists to proceed with construction, and a whole cadre of landscape advocates (*Landschaftsanwälte*) was employed by the Nazis to oversee all kinds of construction projects. Under the direction of Reich Minister for Armaments and Munition Fritz Todt and his advisor, landscape architect and master gardener Alwin Seifert, landscape architects were also involved in the Germanization of occupied territories.[48] Just like the invaded areas were to be "cleansed" of Jewish and local Slavic populations, the landscape was cleansed by changing its character and adapting it to German needs and economic visions. The landscape architects were aware of the experimentation in the camps and the Nazis' genocidal policies, and many of them were complicit and supported Nazi ideology.

In the end, the question remains, how green were the Nazis? This image of the "green Nazis" has been used for different purposes. Some refer to it to damage the reputation of current environmentalist movements, while others highlight it to diminish the monstrosity of the Nazis.[49] The depiction of the Nazis as early environmentalists, and the claim that current nature conversation movements share ideological currents with the Nazis, have stirred up a considerable debate. While this debate does not need to be recounted here in detail, it has in the end produced great insights and contributed to a more complex understanding of Nazi ideology and practice.[50] In the context of food as a science under the Nazis it is worth looking more closely at Darré's interest in alternative farming methods, or more specifically in anthroposophic farming, an examination that will show that the Nazis were indeed a lot more "brown" than "green."

DARRÉ AND BIODYNAMIC FARMING

During his trial in Nuremberg after the war, Richard Walther Darré embellished his affinity with the anthroposophic movement and his alleged support for organic farmers. Anthroposophy is a philosophy put forth by Rudolf Steiner in the 1920s. Steiner argued that a spiritual world existed that could be reached through intuition and imagination. Applied to agriculture, anthroposophic farmers proposed a holistic and natural approach to the soil, rejecting chemical fertilizer and pesticides. Today they are considered early practitioners of organic farming methods. Strict followers of the anthroposophic school also adjusted farm work to astrological signs and constellations. Many Nazi officials watched the movement with suspicion, and some of the followers were threatened with persecution and imprisonment. During the Nuremberg trial, Darré claimed that during his time as the Minister of Food and Agriculture he had protected small-scale anthroposophic farmers from persecution and maintained that he should therefore be understood as a harmless advocate of small peasants rather than a Nazi ideologist.[51] His main concern had been the livelihood and work of small farmers. Darré went so far as to tell the judges that he had become a Nazi Minister against his will and was used by the Nazis for their own political goals. Darré claimed that he had never shared the Nazis' ambitious plans of achieving food autarky and expanding Germany's territory in the East. He also downplayed his original interest in racial sciences and his training in plant and animal breeding that had been so central to the emergence of the Nazis' blood-and-soil ideology. To emphasize his own divergence from the official party line, Darré employed his connections to the biodynamic farm movement. He described how he had been in a constant struggle with other Nazi leaders and was reprimanded when he had allowed small biodynamic farmers to continue their work. He positioned himself as somebody who had protected these farmers from persecution and punishment at the risk of sacrificing his own political career. Darré depicted his ultimate dismissal from the post of Nazi Minister as his final break from Nazi ideas.[52]

In reality, however, Darré, had shown little interest in the movement until the late 1930s. For example, he had dismissed repeated invitations by Eduard Bartsch, a leader of the organic farm movement, to visit a model organic farm. Bartsch believed that organic farming and the independence from chemical fertilizer would contribute to the Nazis' goal of food autarchy and increased self-sufficiency. Furthermore, Bartsch thought that organic family farmers would be perfectly suited settlers in the newly conquered territories. Darré's interest in organic farming at this point was little more than an overall curiosity about the effectiveness of alternative farming methods, rather than an indicator of his support of the movement.[53]

Darré's racial worldview overlapped closely with Nazi ideology.[54] Darré had distinguished himself early on as a scientist of animal breeding. He had written several books and articles on the "Nordic race" and was well connected in right-wing circles. Adopting the findings from his research with animals, he had promoted ways to eliminate racially less valuable people to create a master race that would lead the new greater German Reich. Healthy and racially pure German peasants, in his view, would become the foundation of the German race. Peasants were thus not just the cultural backbone, as agrarian romanticists of the nineteenth century had described them, they were the "life source" and the genetic stock for the new master race. German peasants would also be settled in the newly acquired territories in the East. Darré's ideas were at the heart of the Nazi ideology and remained important until the collapse of the regime. They had heavily influenced Nazi politics and did so even after he had lost his ministerial post.

Other Nazi officials had shown an interest in alternative agriculture long before Darré. Himmler had studied agriculture and promoted a healthy and organic diet. He was not a follower of the Steiner ideology but was interested in the natural approach to farming. He agreed with Darré's understanding of the peasants as the life source of the German race, and like Darré, he believed that peasants would play a leading role in the future of the German Reich. As an early supporter of Darré, Himmler had made him the first Director of the SS Race and Settlement Office (*Rasse- und Siedlungshauptamt*) that oversaw marriage regulations for SS men. Darré's suggested marriage and reproduction regulations aimed at "breeding" future leaders for Germany in Himmler's elite military organization, the SS.

It was another Nazi leader, Rudolf Hess, who crossed the official party line by openly supporting organic farming and followers of anthroposophy.[55] Hess had actually criticized Darré for not doing anything to protect the organic farmers from interference by officials from the *Reichs-Nährstand* (Reich Food Estate).[56] Only in 1941, when Germany's defeat of France had protected Germany from a food blockade similar to World War I was Darré willing to change his tone about alternative farming techniques. He now allowed for some small-scale experimentation with anthroposophic farming and was encouraged when organic farmers produced good results.[57] Darré and other Nazi leaders remained suspicious, however, of the teachings of the Rudolf Steiner school. The anthroposophic farmers' association was disbanded, and some of the leading figures, like Eduard Bartsch, were interrogated. At this point, Darré was critical of the harsh treatment and argued that the farmers should be allowed to work with alternative methods. He wrote to Hitler to inform him of the actions against the leaders. He also confided in Hitler that he had been instructed to deliver only organic produce to the Führer himself, a comment that was intended to garner support for the cause from Hitler.[58] Until the end of the war, organic farmers were allowed to continue farming following their alternative methods.

Some of the anthroposophic farmers also benefited from collaboration with the regime. The concentration camp in Dachau, for example, had an herb garden that was maintained by Franz Lippelt, who was an active follower of anthroposophy. Lippelt employed prisoners from the camp to work in the garden.[59]

After his release from prison in 1950, Darré got in touch with anthroposophic groups and devoted his last couple of years to the cause. His interest at this point might have been genuine, but it certainly does not take away from his contributions to Nazi food and agricultural policy.[60] Authors who depict Darré as an "early green" because of his sympathy for anthroposophic farming have not looked at the historical record critically enough. They misinterpret and overestimate Darré's interest in the Steiner movement in an attempt to portray him in a more positive light.

In general, historical research has shown that the Nazis can hardly be considered forerunners of the environmental movement. While the Nazis' ideology of blood and soil might have suggested a strong connection between the people and the land they inhabited, Nazi agricultural and food policy was anything but green. Hitler's quest for autarky, for example, called for an intensification of agriculture, which stood in clear opposition to nature conversation and environmental stewardship. To increase food production, Hitler demanded that "no square meter of German soil shall remain uncultivated."[61] The Four-Year Plan that prepared Germany for war had also paid little heed to nature conservation. War, territorial expansion, and food autarky clearly took priority over nature conservation or animal protection.

CODA: HITLER'S VEGETARIANISM

In biographies of Adolf Hitler as well as in public media, the notion of Hitler as a vegetarian resurfaces repeatedly. Some food writers and spokesmen for vegetarianism go to great lengths to debunk the "myth" that Hitler was a committed vegetarian while other writers have used Hitler's comments about food to discredit the vegetarian and ecological movement.[62] In the end, it is irrelevant for the understanding of the Nazi period to know whether Hitler was a vegetarian. In the context of food in the Third Reich and Nazi food politics, however, it is interesting to look at Hitler's food habits and how these were used to reinforce certain messages about consumption and the economy overall. Nazi propaganda concerning food was—as chapter 1 has shown—central to the success of the Nazi Party early on and the issue of food remained important for the economy during the 1930s and the war. So what did Nazi propaganda make of Hitler's food habits and his demonstrative love of animals?

Goebbels used Hitler's vegetarianism as propaganda to emphasize Hitler's asceticism and his Spartan way of life. As chapter 2 has shown, during times when food was rationed and Germans were asked to use leftovers or to replace the Sunday roast with root vegetables from their own gardens, it was important to show the *Führer* as someone who had also adjusted his lifestyle, lived economically, and shared the same meals as his compatriots. Goebbels was disturbed by rumors about other Nazi leaders who indulged in elaborate meals at fancy restaurants or drank excessively at private parties.[63] Hitler, however, could be depicted as somebody who never smoked and did not drink any alcohol. He took his simple meals in the company of those closest to him and did not care much about what he ate. During the last years of his life, he did not eat any meat and allegedly became angry when his cook made dishes with beef broth. After this he requested only clear soups and mashed potatoes. But Hitler had not always been a vegetarian. He had eaten plenty of meat in his life and often expressed how much he liked Bavarian food, especially sausages, ham, and liver.

Some writers go to great length to emphasize that Hitler was not a full-fledged vegetarian. He had only turned to a vegetarian diet late in his life, and even then he retained his fondness for nonvegetarian foods. One author seems to know that Hitler only went on "vegetarian binges to cure himself of excessive sweatiness and flatulence."[64] Eager to avoid an association of vegetarianism and Nazism, some food writers stress that vegetarian groups were persecuted by the Nazis and risked their lives when they met in secret.[65] Hitler's stand toward vegetarianism does not have any significance for historical events. Nor does it constitute a paradox that a dictator who oversaw one of the greatest genocides in history might have followed a vegetarian diet and loved animals.[66] Hitler had personal tastes and preferences when it came to food and drink, a fact that does not diminish the monstrosities of his actions.

6

THE HUNGER YEARS AFTER THE WAR

Chapter 2 ended with a description of how hunger arrived in Germany in the winter of 1944–1945. Until the last year of the war, Backe's ration system had worked well and had ensured that most Germans at home had enough to eat. The hunger and social unrest that had occurred during World War I had been prevented, largely because of the exploitation of occupied countries that brought food into the Reich. Between 1939 and 1944, hunger was exported to other countries across Europe. It became the weapon of destruction against unwanted people in the concentration and prison camps, and in the cities and areas destined for exploitation. Germans, at the same time, benefitted from an efficient rationing system and they had been encouraged to change their eating habits and consume what was taken from people in the occupied territories.

When the front started to close in on Germany and enemy soldiers advanced into the Reich in late 1944, food supplies became tighter for Germans as well. The ongoing bombing of cities and the destruction of transportation networks, train stations, and bridges made the distribution of food increasingly difficult. German troops, under orders to feed themselves from the bounty of conquered land in the East, were retreating on all fronts and faced scorched earth and depleted resources on their way back. No plans had been made to supply food for these men once the tide of war had turned. When the soldiers could no longer sustain themselves on their enemy's productive capacities, the need to feed them put immense pressure on German food supplies. Backe responded by cutting all special allowances and adjusting army rations to the same level as rations for civilians. When even those could no longer be ensured, rations for all consumer groups were cut. Even basic foods such as sugar and bread were in short supply. Backe further tightened the already strict control of domestic farm production to get as much from agricultural producers as possible. Even in the rural areas, however, food resources were extremely scarce. The influx of millions of refugees from bombed-out cities and lost eastern territories had dramatically increased the village populations and strained food supplies. With the advance of the Soviet troops, many Germans embarked on a hectic escape from the Red Army. The flight of over six million people from Silesia and East Prussia between fall 1944 and spring 1945 took on chaotic dimensions and led to the doubling or tripling of the population in rural areas.

The inevitable collapse on the German military and food supply front stood in stark contrast to the official propaganda and the ongoing promises made by Goebbels and his staff. Backe reluctantly acknowledged the desperate food situation in his August 29, 1944, report: "It is obvious that the less desirable factors outweigh the favorable factors for a mediocre to good harvest."[1] The adjustments he proposed signaled how critical the situation had become. New regulations cut the use of barley for beer production by half and limited the number of small animals that individual households were allowed to keep. A family could, for example, own only three ducks, three geese, and a small number of chickens or rabbits. All other animals had to be turned in and slaughtered. Every bit of food had to be reserved for human consumption.[2] By the end of February 1945, the regulations became even more restrictive. Ducks or geese could not be kept anymore at all—to save food and help those "who were brought in from the East."[3] Cities were ordered to grow as much produce as possible since the transportation of food to the cities had become extremely difficult. Even the smallest plots and city parks were turned into potato fields and vegetable gardens. In the spring of 1945, half of the fields were left untilled because there were simply not enough hands left to do the necessary farm work. Male agricultural workers of all ages had been drafted and many never returned from the front. Rations for the period from February to April 1, 1945, further reduced daily calories to less than half of what they had been at the beginning of the war. For the next three years, official daily rations remained well below the minimum needed to survive. Hunger had finally arrived in Germany.

NAZI AGRICULTURAL POLICY ON TRIAL IN NUREMBERG

The men in charge of food could do little to alleviate the critical situation in early 1945. The shortage of laborers, the difficulties in transportation, and the great number of refugees who needed to be fed put enormous strain on food supplies. Over the last year of the war, Backe had become increasingly frustrated and desperate, as the letters to his wife testify.[4] He understood that Germany was heading toward a catastrophic collapse, but this recognition did not lead him to question his belief in Hitler and the Nazi cause. In 1945, Backe's devotion to the Nazis' mission was just as strong as it had been in August 1941, when he had rhetorically asked his wife whether there were "others who sacrifice their lives for the mission as much as I do?"[5] Throughout the war, Backe had been plagued by worries, depression, and exhaustion, but he never gave up his belief that he alone would get the job done.[6] In August 1944, he vowed that he would fight until the end. His admiration for and trust in Hitler's abilities were stronger than ever and he confessed to his wife that his: "last thought will be the Reich and its creator the Führer."[7] Backe wondered whether he could have done more or should have been less obsessed about Darré, who had turned from an ally and mentor into a rival.[8] "I accuse myself of not having fought harder. All I saw was the impossible Darré, who destroyed the work I had to do for the people. I have to admit that I wasn't strong enough for this greater and more important task."[9] He prepared his wife for what he considered to be the inevitable—the murder of their four children before they would fall into the hands of the Soviets.[10] In a letter that could be read as a farewell to his wife, he praises her for her strength and her ongoing support of him: "I wish I had your will to live and your resources. . . . It was you alone who strengthened me in my struggles, who supported me when I despaired."[11]

On April 21, 1945, when the Soviet troops had started to attack Berlin in what would be the final battle of the war in Europe, Backe left the city. After Hitler committed suicide on April 30 in his bunker, a new government led by naval commander Karl Dönitz as the head of state took over executive control of the new government at the headquarters in Flensburg. The central task was to negotiate surrender with the Western Allies. But there was little to negotiate. The Allies accepted only unconditional surrender, which took effect on May 8, 1945. All members of the so-called Flensburg government, including Backe who had continued as the Minister of Food, were arrested on May 23 by the Allied Powers. Backe was sent to the American military headquarters in Rheims, France, where he started working on a report to be presented to General Dwight D. Eisenhower, the Supreme Commander of the Allied Forces in Germany. Backe was convinced that the Allies needed his expertise to avoid a large-scale famine. To his surprise, Eisenhower never received him. Instead, the Americans treated Backe like a prisoner and transferred him to a POW camp in Attichy, Francc. Backe was later moved to an internment camp in Ziegenhain near Frankfurt and ended up in the prison in Nuremberg where he was to be put on trial together with other Nazi leaders.

While in the Nuremberg prison, Backe wrote two documents reflecting on his life's work, the "Great Report" (*Grosser Bericht*) and a long letter to his wife that he entitled "A Draft of a Political Testament."[12] In these documents, Backe described his political ideas and his career, and he reflected on his relationships with other Nazi leaders such as Himmler, Darré, and Göring. Backe's tone is not apologetic, and it is free of any feeling of guilt or responsibility for the consequences of his food policy. Backe was convinced that he had done the right thing and did not feel guilty of any war crimes. Backe even claimed that his agricultural and food policy had actually prevented hunger and starvation, not only for Germans, but also for the people in the occupied territories.[13] In the letter to his wife dated January 31, 1946, he defended National Socialism as one of the greatest ideas of all time and relished the accomplishments of Nazi agricultural policy. "I can say without vanity that the agrarian policy based on this idea [National Socialism] was an accomplishment that cannot be erased from history. . . . National Socialism has proved itself right in the area of agriculture."[14] While the Great Report and the Testament could be read as purposeful reflections that would be read by the judges who were going to try him, Backe's spirit comes through as unbroken and self-assured.

Backe was to be tried in the so-called Wilhelmstrasse Trials in Nuremberg, held by the United States against various Nazi ministries in 1947–1948. The trial got its name from the street address of the German Foreign Ministry, located on Wilhelmstrasse in Berlin. It followed the Trials of the Major War Criminals conducted by the International Military Tribunal in 1945–1946 and charged other surviving leaders of the Nazi regime as well as groups of persecutors such as doctors, judges, and economists. The trials took place in the same courthouse in Nuremberg and were held by the Americans. In total, twenty-one members of the various Reich ministries were tried, including two men who had been involved in agricultural and food policy: Richard Walther Darré and Paul Körner.[15] Backe was interrogated twice in preparation for his trial, once in February and once in March 1947, by chief prosecutor Robert Kempner who accused him of authorizing the starvation of masses of Soviet citizens. Backe, however, avoided further scrutiny and a possible verdict from the judges by committing suicide on April 6 in his prison cell. According to his children, there were rumors that he would be deported to the Soviet Union to be tried there.[16] In the last letters to his family, Backe spoke of his suffering, solitude, and hunger in his prison cell. The fear of deportation might have been his main motivation to hang himself, but we will never know what ultimately drove him to take his own life just like his father had done one generation earlier.[17] His suicide allowed him to escape formal justice, and Backe's name and the role he had played for Nazi hunger politics, quickly disappeared from public memory.[18]

Backe's predecessor, the first Nazi Minister of Food and Agriculture, Richard Walther Darré, was alive and had to endure the scrutiny of the persecution. Since Darré had been dismissed from his political post on May 13, 1942, he had had plenty of time to work out his defense and to put his spin on the interpretation of the events. He had been isolated from politics and public attention for three years, during which he had struggled with health problems and depression.[19] The resentment he felt against those people among the Nazi leaders who had disempowered him only grew during that time.[20] For the Nuremberg prosecutors, Darré depicted himself as an outsider of the Nazi elite who had been misunderstood and used by other party officials for their own goals. He told his codefendant Hans-Joachim Riecke before the trial that he planned to "blame Backe for everything."[21] He explained to the judges that he had become minister against his will and claimed that he did not agree with the Nazis' vision and ambition to conquer more lands.[22] Since Backe was not present to describe his close collaboration with Darré during the early years, it was Darré's version of his own role that entered the historical record. This uncritical picture was only revised starting in the late 1990s.[23]

The American judges in Nuremberg found Darré guilty of membership in a criminal organization, atrocities committed against civilian populations, and plunder and spoliation. More specifically, he was held responsible for overseeing discriminatory food rations for Jews, the expropriation of Jewish-owned farmland, "reducing to serfdom hundreds of thousands of Polish and Jewish farmers in the course of the ethnic German settlement," and plunder and destruction in Poland.[24] He was not found guilty, however, of the first and most grievous count, the participation in the planning, preparation, initiation, and waging of wars of aggression and invasion of other countries. His sentence was light; he received only seven years in prison, including those he had already served in Nuremberg. The only other man in charge of agriculture who was tried in Nuremberg, Paul Körner, state secretary in the Four-Year Plan administration, received fifteen years. Körner's sentence was later reduced to ten years, and in 1951, he received amnesty and walked out of prison a free man. Darré was also released early, and he lived from 1950 to1953 in Bad Harzburg where he started writing about organic farming. He died in 1953 of liver cancer.[25]

Backe's second man in the agricultural ministry, Hans-Joachim Riecke, had also been arrested on May 23, 1945, as a member of the Dönitz government. Like Backe, he initially feared deportation to Russia but quickly realized that this was not going to happen. During the months he spent in prison awaiting his trial he temporarily shared a cell with Darré.[26] In the end, Riecke was never put on trial, but served as a witness for the defense of Alfred Rosenberg in the Nuremberg war crime trials.[27] The defense claimed that Riecke's statement would "prove that during the German occupation no Ukrainian or Soviet citizen suffered from hunger."[28] Riecke told the prosecutors that he himself had wanted to help peasants work independently and to serve the needs of the local populations. When asked about the *Hungerplan* and the calculated expropriation of resources from the Soviet Union, Riecke confirmed that the Eastern territories were expected to feed German troops and to provide supplies for Germany: "Approximately two thirds of the food resources from the occupied territories were used by the *Wehrmacht*. The remainder was transported to Germany to provide food for the constantly growing number of foreign workers."[29] There was no denial of the practice of a Nazi agricultural and food policy and its murderous effect on Soviet and Polish citizens and POWs. Riecke was released from prison on March 23, 1949, and pursued a successful career in the Alfred Töpfer Company, a leading organization in international grain trade. He died in 1986 at the age of eighty-seven.

HUNGER AND DEMOCRACY

After Germany's unconditional surrender on May 8, 1945, the Allies faced an enormous task in Central Europe. Most of the continent lay in shambles. Cities and urban areas had been hit hard by air strikes and were largely destroyed. All over Europe, much of the agricultural land was rendered unusable, and even where fields were fertile and productive, there were not enough hands left to bring in the harvest. Millions of refugees, survivors from concentration camps, POWs, and displaced persons depended on the Allies for food, shelter, and a return to their original homeland. A large-scale hunger crisis was looming over Europe.

In Germany, the loss of the Eastern territories had deprived the country of its most arable land and of the largest and most productive farms. The doors to Germany's "breadbasket" (*Kornkammer*) and "potato cellar" were shut—and would never reopen again. Everywhere in Germany, food production was down because of a serious shortage of chemical fertilizer, seeds, and machinery. To make things worse, the first two postwar winters were unusually cold and there was not enough coal or firewood to keep people warm. Daily average food rations were down more than 40 percent compared to rations at the beginning of the war. According to official estimates of the French occupying power, people in the city of Stuttgart had to survive on an average of 793 calories a day.[30]

Access to food varied greatly from region to region. In industrial and urban centers, food was especially hard to come by. People in the cities resorted to self-help, grew their own food on even the smallest lot, and kept chickens or rabbits on balconies and a pig in the basement. They went on frequent forages into the countryside to look for anything edible that could be brought home to hungry families. Many took the "potato trains" or the "calorie express" to travel from their homes in Cologne or Hamburg to the agricultural regions in Bavaria where they bartered with anything they had. When this was not enough to feed a family, people resorted to stealing coal from trains and potatoes from the fields. The black market had become the most powerful economic force, where everything could be found for horrendously high prices. About one-quarter of all manufactured foods was traded on the black market. Money—the *Deutsche Reichsmark*—had completely lost its value, and American cigarettes were the most valuable currency. The occupation authorities could do little to stop illegal activities. Even in the Soviet zone, where people faced harsh punishment if caught in the act, many crossed the line of what would be considered legal. After another cold winter and a meager potato harvest, food supplies reached their lowest level in the summer of 1947. Overall food production in Germany was at only 25 percent of the level of 1938–1939.[31]

The small quantity and low quality of food had negative effects especially on the health of children. Prompted by the suffering, Americans started to send CARE packages to West Germany and other European countries. The first shipments destined for Germany arrived in July 1946 at the port of Bremen for distribution to German families in need. The packages were sponsored by individual American senders and contained preserved meat, margarine and lard, dried fruit, chocolate, milk powder, coffee, and other food items. Through the aid organization CARE (Cooperative for American Remittances to Europe), over 82,000 tons of food were sent to West Germany over the next decade and brought welcome relief to many families.[32]

The food crisis represented the greatest challenge for the victorious Allies in the first postwar years. All four powers agreed that food production and supplies had to be increased immediately, but the former wartime Allies had very different ideas on how to go about it. The differences escalated over questions of food and agricultural policies. At the first postwar conference in Potsdam in July 1945, Germany had been divided into four zones of occupation—the Soviet zone in the east, the British zone in northern Germany, and the American occupation zone in the southern parts of Germany. France received a small area in the west along the French border. The Eastern territories of Prussia, Upper Silesia, and parts of Pomerania were temporarily placed under Polish jurisdiction, an arrangement that became a permanent loss of Germany's most important agricultural lands. To compensate the Soviet Union for its heavy losses, the Western powers agreed to deliver 10 percent of the industrial capacity of their zones to the Soviet Union. The agricultural sector was excluded from the war reparations since that would have disturbed the fragile food supplies even further.[33] Even so, the Potsdam regulations had a detrimental effect on agricultural production. Major industrial factories that produced fertilizers were shut down and farmers lacked machinery, farm tools, and seeds to increase production.[34] It would take several years for domestic agricultural production to reach prewar levels.

The effort to respond to the crisis was hampered by the growing confrontation of the two new superpowers. In the frigid climate of the emerging Cold War ideologies, the collaboration between the Americans and Soviets, as initially envisioned in the war conference of Yalta in February 1945, became increasingly unrealistic. The economic and political priorities of the United States and the Soviet Union were incompatible and they collided in the realm of agricultural and food policy. The Soviet Union demanded compensation for the terrible suffering caused by the German invasion and three years of brutal warfare and immediately started to take anything that was movable from their occupation zone. Great Britain, in contrast, was primarily interested in security from future German attacks, while the United States, the new economic superpower, envisioned a quick German recovery to establish a free European and global market.

The U.S. Military Governor in Germany, Lucius Clay, warned the government in Washington that the question of food supplies for the western zones was closely linked to a healthy industrial recovery and had to be tackled immediately. Underfed workers were less productive since they had less physical energy and spent too much time searching for food. Industrial workers in the Ruhr area threatened to strike and social unrest was expected to break out in many areas. Immediate financial aid for Germany was thus imperative to ensure social peace and an overall economic recovery. Clay explained this connection between food supplies, work productivity, and the European recovery to gain support from Washington for financial aid to Germany: "Without food we cannot produce coal; without coal we cannot support the transportation industry; without coal we cannot produce the fertilizer necessary to improve future food supply. Only food can prime the pump."[35] Clay also stressed the political dimension of hunger, since "hungry people do not make good democrats."[36] According to Clay, hunger stood in the way of the formation of a democratic and capitalist Europe and it was therefore in the interest of the United States to provide financial aid to Germany:

> There is no choice between becoming a Communist on 1,500 calories and a believer in democracy on 1,000 calories. It is my sincere belief,

> that our proposed ration allowance in Germany will not only defeat our objective in middle Europe but will pave the road to a Communist Germany.[37]

In his report on the food conditions in Germany, Clay stated that there simply could be "no growth of democracy among people fighting for food and for the maintenance of life itself."[38] A strong and economically viable Germany seemed to be in America's best interest, since nobody in Washington wanted the American taxpayers to pay for German food and support in the long run.

This rationale also informed the passing of the Marshall Plan or the European Recovery Program in 1947. Financial help started to pour into Western Europe in the forms of loans and grants beginning in 1948. The Soviet Union rejected the American interference and economic oversight that was tied to the financial aid and pressured Eastern European countries not to participate. In the end, aid was given only to democratic governments and none of the communist countries in Eastern Europe were included in the recovery program. In the spirit of the Truman doctrine, Greece and Turkey were the first to receive American financial aid. Over the next four years, $14 billion was pumped into Western Europe. According to the American planners, the aid would create a stable Western Europe and would provide the best protection against the spread of communism.

The American effort to rebuild Germany was a considerable change from earlier visions for the defeated country. Some had called for a more punitive treatment of Germany or believed that Germany needed to pay for its recovery on its own. One of the options that Americans had considered before the end of the war was the so-called Morgenthau plan. U.S. Secretary of the Treasury Henry Morgenthau had suggested in 1944 that Germany should be deindustrialized to ensure that the country would never again rebuild military strength. The conversion of Germany into a land of peasants and shepherds would enable a democratization of Germany similar to the American version of the small independent family farmer who formed the basis of a republican state and democratic government. The Morgenthau plan for industrial disarmament, however, was abandoned because it ran counter to the idea of a politically strong Europe in the future that was needed to establish peace and stability.

The Soviets also understood the political risks associated with the widespread experience of hunger and quickly initiated changes in their occupation zone. Urbanites were organized to help rural folks with the harvest and secure food. Workers in critical industries received special food rations to increase productivity, and all incomes and prices were fixed. The government aggressively suppressed any black market activity, but with limited success. The Soviets' main priority, however, was the restructuring of farm sizes and the breaking of the power of the old landed elites.[39] The Communist government hastily initiated a change in landownership by implementing a radical land reform.[40] Properties of all large landowners with more than one hundred hectares and those of all Nazi war criminals were expropriated. The land was then to be distributed among the landless in small parcels of five to ten hectares. This land was free of prior debts or other obligations, but a price—the equivalent of one year's harvest—was to be paid by the new owner in money or kind over the next ten to twenty years. By mid-1946, the land commissions had completed their work. Two and a half years later, one-third of all agricultural and forest land had been expropriated, a total of 3,225,364 hectares or 13,699 properties. A total of 209,000 new peasant farms with an average size of eight hectares had been created and another 120,000 grants of land had been added to existing small farms. Most agricultural land was now held in units of five to twenty hectares. Farms larger than one hundred hectares had declined from one-third of all farms to 11 percent by 1950.[41]

The Communist government celebrated the land reform as a great success. It had demolished the old social structure in one stroke and had destroyed the large landowners' power. With the redistribution of land to the landless, a new social order had been created consisting of a class of small peasants who were heavily indebted to the new regime.[42] Economically, however, the land reform was far from successful. Fall planning was disrupted, and much of the property of the more successful famers had been expropriated or they had left the occupation zone for the West. There was great mismanagement of funds, seeds, and livestock, and widespread looting further aggravated the situation. Many of the newly created farms were far too small to be profitable, and the overall agricultural output declined dramatically. Modernization or technological improvements were stalled, since the newly landed peasants did not have the means nor the state support for investment in machines. A great number of plots were left untilled and quickly abandoned by the new owners who could not make a living on the small plots of land. Over the years, many farmers returned their land to the state, fled to the West, or left farming all together.[43]

In 1952, the East German government announced the next step toward socialist agriculture and toward the transformation of peasants into "socialist personalities," the collectivization drive.[44] Agricultural Producer's Cooperatives (*Landwirtschaftliche Produktionsgenossenschaften*, or LPGs) were founded that peasants were supposed to join voluntarily. Most peasants, however, resented collectivization and would rather give up farming than join the cooperatives. By the late 1950s, the governments used pressure and intimidation to force peasants to comply, with the result that the percentage of land included in cooperatives rose from 37.8 percent in 1959 to 84.4 percent in 1960.[45] According to official statements, the collectivization drive and "socialist transformation of agriculture" were completed by the summer of 1960.[46]

In the western parts of Germany, the social and rural structures were largely left intact. At first, there had been talk about a redistribution of land, but no direct measures were taken. The Western occupation powers looked for ways to ensure a fast restoration of the economy and the quick setup of a democratic administration that would manage agricultural production and food distribution. Any social disruption—like the massive restructuring of landownership—had to be avoided at all costs. Since Germany's agricultural production was considered crucial for a rapid recovery of Europe overall, the new authorities were careful with any changes in the existing social order. The properties of large landowners were not expropriated and only a very small percentage of the land changed hands.

The different paths in agriculture taken by the occupation powers paved the way for a division of Germany into two separate states. The confrontation between the United States and the Soviet Union found its foremost expression in agricultural and food policies. The "iron curtain" had descended in the middle of Europe and would affect economic developments for the next fifty years.

FOOD POLICY IN THE OCCUPATION ZONES

In all four zones, the occupation authorities continued the rationing system first introduced by Backe in 1939.[47] When the daily calorie supply dropped drastically and hit bottom in the first postwar winter, each zone set up its own infrastructure and administration for agriculture and food distribution. The American Office of Military Government for Germany (OMGUS) swiftly delegated administrative and political authority to the Germans in their zone. A central office for food and agriculture under the direction of Hermann Dietrich[48] was charged to ensure an equal distribution of food across the occupation zone. The British established in their zone a Central Office for Food and Agriculture (*Zentralamt für Landwirtschaft und Ernährung*, ZEL) that oversaw the collection, delivery, distribution, and import of food. Hans Schlange-Schöningen[49] was appointed the head of the organization. In the British occupation zone, the Nazis' administrative body, the Reich Food Estate (RNS), remained in place to oversee food production and distribution. Membership in the RNS was no longer compulsory and the organization took on a more democratic structure, but many former staff continued to be employed in the food administration. The RNS was formally dissolved in January 1948.[50] Just like the Americans in their zone, the British quickly abandoned the idea of land reform. Hans Schlange had himself been the owner of the large land estate Schöningen in Pomerania and had fled to the West in early 1945. He had no interest in changing the structure of landownership or in pursuing a strict denazification of large landowners as was done by the Soviets.[51]

The French occupying power also established a central agency to administer food policy in their zone. The collaboration between French occupiers and German administrators turned out to be more difficult. One of the most contentious issues was the support of the French troops with food from the occupation zone, a practice that stretched the already scarce resources even more. Both the American and British occupation powers imported all food needed to support their troops. In January 1947, the British and the American zone merged into one united zone and combined their administrative offices. Hans Schlange-Schöningen functioned as the director for the food administration in the so-called Bizonia. This way, work could be coordinated more efficiently and food delivery problems could be solved in collaboration.

The foremost task for the central offices was to increase food production in the zone. Despite the good intentions, however, conflicts arose between German, American, and British authorities and between peasants and consumer interests. The chronic shortages continued and many of the regulations were met with resistance. Stories circulated of peasants trading potatoes for Persian carpets and exploiting the situation by enriching themselves via the black market. Peasants refused the American order to deliver food at low prices and resisted the call to minimize their herds and grow more grain. In fact, peasants would rather kill their animals than turn them over to the administration, a behavior the Americans likened to sabotage.[52] American authorities grew increasingly irritated with the peasants' reluctance to deliver. An enraged U.S. Military Governor Clay even threatened to "let people starve" if Germans did not step up to solve their agricultural problems themselves:

> Maybe we had better let people starve if they don't run their affairs better than that. I am not going to get too worried about it. The point I am trying to make is I am not willing to bring food in to replace food that Germans didn't plant which they could have planted. Or to replace food that goes to animals. . . . I think we might as well tell them so, but think we ought [to] . . . bring home to the German people that the reason of their failure to get food is their own administrative failure to do the maximum with what they have.[53]

Tensions between the city and the countryside and between the occupation powers and the German administration escalated over the issue of food. Many Germans, however, saw the hunger crisis as a result of punitive treatment by the occupation powers, rather than the outcome of peasant behavior. In rural areas, many farmers stepped up to help refugees and bombed-out families. They took refugees into their homes, shared meals, and distributed potatoes and eggs in return for help in the fields. The resistance was directed against German government officials and the Allies. Schlange-Schöningen was often caught in the middle of the conflicting interests and had to maneuver between what looked like egoistic peasants, ungrateful Germans, or overly demanding occupation powers. When the Central Office—upon the insistence of the Allies—issued the so-called food pantry law (*Speisekammergesetz*) in January 1948 that required all food producers, merchants, and restaurants to give full disclosure of all their food stocks, the public debate and open resistance to the "emergency law against the peasants" reached another level. Only a very small number of questionnaires were returned and it became clear that collaboration had reached an impasse. A polemic speech by a German politician—Johannes Semler—in Bizonia exemplified the tensions:

> Americans send us corn and chicken feed and we have to pay for it dearly. They don't give it to us for free. We have to pay for it in dollars from German work and German exports and we are even expected to be grateful. German politicians should stop saying thank you for these food deliveries.[54]

Semler, the Executive Director of Economics for the combined British and American zone, was dismissed on January 27, 1948, shortly after his inflammatory speech. In March, Ludwig Erhard was elected to replace him as Director of Economics for Bizonia. On both sides, the more reasonable voices prevailed, and most people understood the political implications of the critical food situation. Clay's personal advisor, James L. Pollock, chose a conciliatory tone and acknowledged how difficult it was to overcome existing difficulties.[55] The fear of communist inroads and of endangering the democratic project eventually convinced the U.S. government in Washington to agree to more food imports to alleviate the situation in Germany. This was only supposed to be a short-term solution, while a bigger plan was needed to ensure Germany's and Europe's recovery in the long run.

A turning point in the postwar economic development was the currency reform in the Western zones. On June 20, 1948, the *Deutsche Mark* replaced the old currency, the German *Reichsmark*. Everybody received forty Deutsche Mark. All old bank notes had to be deposited in order to exchange them for the new currency. From one day to the next, the Reichsmark had become useless. The currency reform had been planned for several months by the Economic Council of Bizonia under the leadership of Ludwig Erhard, but the actual date was publicly announced only two days before its implementation. In the weeks after the currency reform, Erhard eliminated all price controls and ended the food-rationing system. The food ration card that had dominated the lives of consumers for the past nine years had become obsolete.

The immediate effect of the currency reform was dramatic. The hoarding of food came to an end overnight. Peasants delivered their products and store shelves were filled with a variety of food items that had not been seen in many years. Prices went up immediately, and the better prices seemed to have boosted peasant production from one day to the next.[56] Gone were the shortages characteristic of the weeks before the reform, and the bartering of goods disappeared completely. It seemed as if the whole country, not just the peasants, had changed with the new currency. Workers showed up for work, since they did not need to spend hours foraging for food and were paid in money that had value and could be used to buy food items. With the higher prices, peasants had incentives to produce more and sell their food in stores instead of scaling back production or trading on the black market. Within a year, both food production and industrial output increased exponentially.

The euphoria that followed the currency reform was not shared by everybody and faded considerably over the next few months. Many consumers could not afford to pay the higher prices. An egg, for example, cost five times as much as it had the day before the currency reform. Overall, food prices rose by 18 percent over the next five months. At the same time, peasants faced economic uncertainty with the increased demand for quality, the new competition and the high prices they had to pay for farm machinery.

The currency reform also caused another major food crisis, this time in the city of Berlin. The Soviet occupation power, enraged by the unilateral step in the Western zones, immediately responded with a currency reform in their zone, and then proceeded to block off all roads to Berlin. Neither people nor goods were allowed in or out of Berlin. With the blockade, the Soviets hoped to put pressure on the Western powers to agree on Berlin's status as a free city. The blockade lasted almost an entire year, from June 24, 1948, to May 12, 1949. The American response to the pressure was quite different from the one anticipated by the Soviets. When all roads were blocked to Berlin, the United States started one of the greatest food aid and rescue programs in history, the Berlin airlift. Over the next eleven months, Americans transported all food that was necessary for survival, plus coal and other items needed by the two million Berliners, to the city by air. Airplanes—affectionately dubbed "raisin bombers" or "candy poppers"—dropped tons of food onto streets of the city and into the hands of grateful Germans. Berliners did not starve, even though the city was completely cut off from all trade with its surroundings. When the Soviets gave up the blockade almost one year later, their defeat in the first battle of the Cold War was sealed, while the Americans had cemented their honorary place as saviors in German minds.

The conflicts between the occupation powers, German authorities, and peasants could only be solved in the context of the integration of the farm sector into the new industrial society. With the new economic system and the liberalization of the market, a new era for farming had begun. The old ways of farming had to make way for rationalization and modernization. Small farms were unprofitable and would have to be given up, just as lifestyles would have to change. For German food politicians in the young *Bundesrepublik*, the most urgent dilemma was the gap between prices for agricultural and industrial products. Low price levels remained in place for many agricultural products, while industrial goods were subject to the market that sent prices soaring.[57] This problem, too, would be solved in the context of an overall dramatic European development over the next ten years. The shrinking farm population produced ever more food—and the successful European economic integration in the 1950s would quickly lead to an abundance of food for most people in Western Europe. Rationing cards and substitute food would become a distant memory, while other food habits first introduced under Nazi agricultural policy—most notably the *Eintopf*—would remain a staple of the German cuisine.

OUT OF SCARCITY

After the currency reform, Germany's economic recovery proceeded so quickly that it exceeded even the most optimistic expectations. Within a few years, food consumption had reached prewar levels. Financial aid had started arriving in Germany in early 1948 in the context of the European Recovery Program (ERP), and West Germany alone would receive $2 billion in aid over the next five years. Most of the money paid for the import of goods. The American aid was also used to establish counterpart funds that provided loans to private companies and enabled investment in industry. The Marshall Plan aid supported Germany's economic recovery, but it was not the main driving force. The recovery had already started before the money arrived, and Marshall Plan funds made up only a small percentage of the overall national income.[58] The psychological and political effects of the Marshall Plan, however, were certainly dramatic.

The ERP financed by the United States increased the presence of American products in Europe and tied the West closer to the United States. In the growing confrontation between the two superpowers, Western Europeans increasingly trusted their new powerful ally. The Americans were credited with securing social peace in Europe, and they had helped bring an end to the austerity. In comparison, people under the Soviet sphere of influence had to wait much longer for an overall economic recovery. The growth of Eastern European (and East German) economics lagged behind countries in the West for the entire duration of the Cold War. The economic disparity would become one of the triggers for the upheaval of Eastern European citizens against their regimes and would ultimately lead to the dismantling of the Berlin Wall and the end of the Cold War in 1989.

In Western Europe, living standards rose quickly, and most people found work in the booming industry. Even peasants who had to give up farming participated in the dramatic economic growth. The fear of "losing" the peasantry to the right spectrum of the political landscape because of the massive social change, as it had happened during the economic crisis of the late 1920s, did not materialize due to the growing prosperity among all Germans. Ludwig Erhard, Minister of Economics in Konrad Adenauer's first West German government, had promised to bring "prosperity for all" ("*Wohlstand für alle*"), and he could successfully keep his promise. In the 1950s, Germans ate more meat and poultry, they indulged in butter and other fats, and they consumed more alcohol—all signs of widespread prosperity. The economic recovery seemed "miraculous" to outside observers, and the term economic miracle or *Wirtschaftswunder*, coined in the late 1950s, has since come to signify a dramatic economic recovery.

During the 1950s, the distinctions between rural and urban populations diminished. Many farmers gave up farming as their main income, but instead of selling the land, their families stayed on their small farm, while the men took jobs in nearby factories, and farmed in the evening or on the weekends. In many cases, women remained the only ones on the farm working the land.[59] German food habits and lifestyles changed dramatically. Symbolic for the new dishes and recipes were new ingredients such as ketchup adapted from other countries, especially the United States. Exotic fruits and hitherto unavailable luxury items became more common and started to appear regularly on German tables.[60]

In Germany, a "wave of gluttony" ("*Fresswelle*") followed the hunger years of the 1940s.[61] Small *Tante Emma* or mom-and-pop shops were replaced by supermarkets and large grocery stores that offered all kinds of food at affordable prices. Branding and marketing became the way to do business. Consumerism replaced the habits of food rationing and *Sparsamkeit* (frugality or thriftiness) that had characterized German households for such a long time. Eating habits also changed with the introduction of new food-processing technologies such as canning and freezing.[62] Sweet corn, peas, and spinach could now be bought in a can and were available year-round. Deep freezers were purchased by private households and allowed produce to taste fresh even when it did not come directly from the field or the farm. By the mid-1950s, the consumption of the once omnipresent potato had declined significantly, since many other foods were available and brought variety to German cuisine. The cycle of food, increased consumerism, and greater productivity led to a remarkable overall economic growth in West Germany.

East Germany, or the German Democratic Republic as it was called after 1949, experienced an economic recovery as well, albeit at a slower pace. Here, food rationing ended only in 1958, some ten years after it had disappeared in West Germany. While East Germany's economic growth in the 1960s was impressive and robust compared with other Eastern European economic trends, it did not eliminate the visible signs of food shortages, including long lines in front of grocery stores and the limited availability of more exotic or luxury foods. In these communist societies, a dual consumer society existed, in which few privileged could buy most things in specially designated shops, while the vast majority of the people had access only to what was offered in the state-owned general stores.

Another trend in food and agricultural policy in the early 1950s that would dramatically affect Germany's economic growth was the development of a common European market.[63] The fragile food system after the war and the hostile climate of the Cold War had brought back calls for increased self-sufficiency in food—this time on a European level. The first form of European integration had taken place in the coal and steel industry, and the successful collaboration of the six participating European countries (West Germany, France, Belgium, the Netherlands, Italy, and Luxembourg) became a model for the advocates of a common agricultural and food policy. France, for example, had an interest in collaborating with Germany to sell the food it produced, while Germany would be able to sell its agricultural machinery in return. It became clear, however, that the agricultural sector was much harder to integrate than the coal and steel industry. The agrarian systems that existed across Europe differed dramatically in terms of land sizes, climates, structure of ownership, and customs. A common policy that would address and satisfy all participants seemed very far off. Despite these difficulties, the negotiations proceeded that resulted in the signing of the Treaty of Rome in March 1957 and brought into existence the European Economic Community (EEC).[64]

The Treaty of Rome spelled out common policies for agriculture. At the heart of the agreement was the concern for increased agricultural productivity, the security of food supplies, income security for farmers, and reasonable prices for consumers.[65] A common market for agricultural products was to be established over the next twelve to fifteen years. The European Common Agricultural Policy (CAP) was established ahead of schedule, and by the mid-1960s most agricultural products were part of the common market. The success was considerable, and its main goal, the sufficiency of food supplies, was accomplished. In fact, since production of food grew faster than consumption, the scarcity was soon replaced by an overabundance of food. The market regulations ensured high prices for farm products and incentivized farmers to produce more and more even if the market was saturated. By the 1970s, overproduction of food had become the biggest issue for the European community and manifested itself in what critics called enormous "butter mountains" and "milk lakes."[66] This represented a dramatic change from the scarcity and hunger of the postwar years.

EPILOGUE

Food and food politics played a major role in the history of Germany during the tumultuous first half of the twentieth century. From the food crisis during World War I, to the deportation of hunger during World War II, and finally to the "miraculous recovery" in the 1950s, German society underwent dramatic changes in a relatively short span of time. This book follows these changes, particularly during the Third Reich when food politics became instrumental in the murderous actions of the regime. The importance of food as a weapon is certainly nothing unique to German history. Armies in world history have always withheld any food supplies they could from enemy forces, and in times of war, most governments around the world depend on adequate supplies at home to ensure social and political stability. But the way food politics played out in Germany during the Nazi period was remarkable in many ways, and deserves close attention.

While this book focuses largely on Nazi hunger politics, the sociocultural dimension of food is interesting as well. Starting in the 1950s, German society was profoundly transformed, and the hunger years were replaced by a "wave of gluttony" (*Freßwelle*) and abundance. New foods were introduced, and the arrival of "guest workers" from Southern Europe brought new cuisines to Germany that became so popular and widespread that they forever changed what Germans ate. For young Germans at the beginning of the twenty-first century, Italian pizza, Greek food, and Turkish *Döner Kebab* are as familiar as *bratwurst* and beer. Pasta and potatoes are equally important as starches, just as Italian Chianti rivals

Becks beer in popularity in the omnipresent neighborhood bar (*Kneipe*). The dreaded turnip, so symbolic of the hunger years, has found its way back into German kitchens, this time as part of an alternative artisan or organic food movement that emphasizes local produce and responds to the powerful trend of globalization. Food justice movements draw attention to questions of production and distribution, and discussions are held about genetically modified products, a practice watched with a lot more suspicion in Europe than in the United States. Health scares like the "foot-and-mouth" disease outbreak in 2001 among cattle caused a temporary agricultural crisis affecting how Germans thought about raising cattle and eating meat. Regional growers, organic grocery stores, and food bought directly from the farm all have a small but growing share of today's food market in Germany.

Less than 2 percent of the total workforce today is actively involved in agriculture, but farming and rural lifestyles are still considered to have great cultural value for Germany and receive generous state support. Overall, agricultural politics have lost their prominent and socially explosive place in the political landscape, and only occasionally do the protests of small French farmers in front of McDonald's restaurants make headlines in the news. European agricultural politics are still criticized for their tendency to create a prosperous "fortress" that does not let outsiders in, but food and food politics have became a lot less controversial in German society. A new normalcy has replaced the tumultuous years and features a food regime that is in many ways more open, diverse, and democratic than the system in the first half of the twentieth century.

NOTES

INTRODUCTION

1. In 1915, the Prussian Ministry for Culture had introduced *Sütterlin* to replace the various old German cursive scripts. The script was taught in German schools for a few years, until the Nazis banned it along with all other Gothic scripts and replaced them with Latin-type letters in 1935.

2. See Robert G. Moeller, *War Stories: The Search for a Usable Past in the Federal Republic of Germany* (Berkeley: University of California Press, 2001) for his examination of how war stories were told in postwar Germany. See also Mary Fullbrook, *A Small Town Near Auschwitz: Ordinary Nazis and the Holocaust* (Oxford: Oxford University Press, 2012) for her examination of a Nazi official, Udo Klausa, who depicted himself as a bystander after the war. Fullbrook's own personal entanglement with the story—Klausa was a family friend—makes her rich analysis even more powerful.

3. See the personal collection of Herbert Backe (*Nachlass Herbert Backe*, cited as NL Backe) in the Federal Archives in Koblenz Germany (cited as BAK).

4. There is also a great market for movies about families of perpetrators during and after the war. This outpouring in literature and film can be understood as a new openness of the third generation to talk about their grandparents' deeds. Others interpret this surge in third-generation literature as the result of a new ignorance and a mentality of "moving on" among a young generation of Germans who feel no longer guilty themselves about Germany's past. See also the recent TV series *Unsere Mütter, Unsere Väter* (literally "our mothers, our fathers") that tells the story of five German friends during World War II. The broadcasting provoked a passionate controversy about the portrayal of the Nazis as "others" and different from most "ordinary" Germans.

5. Conversation with Backe siblings, December 21, 2007.

6. Ursula was in contact with Anna Bramwell, who wrote a book about R. W. Darré. See Anna Bramwell, *Blood and Soil: Richard Walther Darré and Hitler's "Green Party"* (Abbotsbrook: Kensal Press, 1985). The families maintained friendly relations over the years and the Backes told me that Armgard's daughter stayed as an au pair with the Bramwells in England. Ursula Backe was also willing to talk to historians Horst Gies and Joachim Lehmann, two other authors whose work is cited repeatedly in this book. Gustavo Corni and Horst Gies, *Brot—Butter—Kanonen. Die Ernährungswirtschaft in Deutschland unter der Diktatur Hitlers* (Berlin: Akademie Verlag, 1997), and Joachim Lehmann, "Herbert Backe—Technokrat und Agrarideologe," in *Die Braune Elite II. 21 Weitere Biographische Skizzen*, eds. Ronald Smelzer, Enrico Syring, and Rainer Zitelmann (Darmstadt: Wissenschaftliche Buchgesellschaft, 1993), 1–12. Bertold Alleweldt wrote his master's thesis on Backe in 2000. The thesis was published in 2011. See Bertold Alleweldt, *Herbert Backe—Eine politische Biographie* (Berlin: Wissenschaftlicher Verlag, 2011). Ursula Backe also talked to historian Susanne Heim. See Götz Aly and Susanne Heim, *Vordenker der Vernichtung. Auschwitz und die deutschen Pläne für eine neue europäische Ordnung*, 2nd ed. (Frankfurt: Fischer Taschenbuch Verlag, 1993).

7. See Hans Deetjen's notes in Bundesarchiv Koblenz, personal collection Darré (signature BAK NL 1094 I 65a).

8. Gesine Gerhard, "Food and Genocide: Nazi Agrarian Food Policy in the Occupied Territories of the Soviet Union," *Contemporary European History* 18, no. 1 (2009): 45–65.

9. Joachim Radkau and Frank Uekötter, eds., *Naturschutz und Nationalsozialismus* (Frankfurt: Campus Verlag, 2003) and Franz-Josef Brüggemeier, Mark Cioc, Thomas Zeller, eds., *How Green Were the Nazis? Nature, Environment, and Nation in the Third Reich* (Athens: Ohio University Press, 2005).

10. Frank Uekötter, *The Green and the Brown: A History of Conservation in Nazi Germany* (Cambridge: Cambridge University Press, 2006).

11. See most importantly the detailed study by Gustavo Corni and Horst Gies, *Brot—Butter—Kanonen*, 1997. See also the new scholarship on the "Nazi diet" by Corinna Treitel, "Nature and the Nazi Diet," *Food and Foodways* 17 (2009): 139–58.

12. Bramwell, *Blood and Soil*; Joachim Lehmann, "Herbert Backe," Corni and Gies, *Brot—Butter—Kanonen.*

13. Susanne Heim, *Kalorien, Kautschuk, Karrieren. Pflanzenzüchtung und Landwirtschaftliche Forschung in Kaiser-Wilhelm-Instituten, 1933–1945* (Göttingen: Wallstein Verlag, 2003); Gerhard, "Food and Genocide"; and Alleweldt, *Herbert Backe.*

14. Issues first raised by Christian Gerlach, *Krieg, Ernährung, Völkermord. Deutsche Vernichtungspolitik im Zweiten Weltkrieg* (Zürich: Pendo Verlag, 2001), and Götz Aly and Susanne Heim, *Vordenker der Vernichtung. Auschwitz und die deutschen Pläne für eine neue europäische Ordnung*, 2nd ed. (Frankfurt: Fischer Taschenbuch Verlag, 1993).

15. Timothy Snyder, *Bloodlands: Europe between Hitler and Stalin* (New York: Basic Books, 2010).

16. Christian Streit, *Keine Kameraden. Die Wehrmacht und die sowjetischen Kriegsgefangenen, 1941–1945* (Stuttgart: Deutsche Verlagsanstalt, 1978). Streit's study published some forty years ago remains the authoritative examination of the topic and little has been added to the topic since then.

17. Susanne Heim, Carola Sachse, and Mark Walker, eds., *The Kaiser Wilhelm Society under National Socialism* (New York: Cambridge University Press, 2009), and Bernd Gausemeier, *Natürliche Ordnungen und politische Allianzen. Biologische und biochemische Forschung an Kaiser-Wilhelm-Instituten, 1933–1945* (Göttingen: Wallstein Verlag, 2005).

18. Frank Uekötter, *The Green and the Brown*, and Franz-Josef Brüggemeier, *How Green Were the Nazis?*

19. Daniela Münkel, *Nationalsozialistische Agrarpolitik und Bauernalltag* (Frankfurt: Campus Verlag, 1996), and Gustavo Corni, *Hitler and the Peasants: Agrarian Policy of the Third Reich, 1930–1939* (New York: Berg, 1990).

20. Some of the findings of my research have been published in the following journal articles and book chapters: "Breeding Pigs and People for the Third Reich: Richard Walter Darré's Agrarian Ideology," in *How Green Were the Nazis? Nature, Environment, and Nation in the Third Reich*, eds. Franz-Josef Brüggemeier, Marc Cioc, and Thomas Zeller (Athens: Ohio University Press, 2005), 129–46; Gerhard, "Food and Genocide"; "Food as a Weapon: Agricultural Sciences and the Building of a Greater German Empire," *Food, Culture and Society* 14, no. 3 (2011): 335–51; and "Richard Walther Darré—Naturschützer oder 'Rassenzüchter'?" in *Naturschutz und Nationalsozialismus*, eds. Joachim Radkau and Frank Uekötter (Frankfurt: Campus Verlag, 2003), 257–72.

1. NO MORE TURNIPS

1. Belinda Davis, *Home Fires Burning: Food, Politics and Everyday Life in World War I Berlin* (Chapel Hill: University of North Carolina Press, 2000), 12.

2. Hans-Jürgen Teuteberg, "Food Provisioning on the German Home Front, 1914–1918," in *Food and War in Twentieth Century Europe*, eds. Ina Zweiniger-Bargielowska, Rachel Duffett, and Alain Drouard (Surrey, England: Ashgate, 2011), 59–72.

3. Davis, *Home Fires Burning*, 22.

4. Davis, *Home Fires Burning*, 23.

5. Teuteberg, "Food Provisioning on the German Home Front," 61.

6. David Welch, *Germany, Propaganda and Total War* (New Brunswick, NJ: Rutgers University Press, 2000), 105.

7. Arnulf Scriba, "Der 'Kohlrübenwinter' 1916/17," *Lebendiges Museum Online, Deutsches Historisches Museum*, September 8, 2014. Accessed November 22, 2014, www.dhm.de/lemo/html/wk1/kriegsverlauf/steckrue/index.html.

8. The term describes a political truce between the Social Democratic Party and other political parties in the German parliament during World War I. The Social Democrats supported the government because many believed it was their patriotic duty. They also feared repression and hoped that by cooperating with the government they would achieve political reforms after the war.

9. Welch, *Germany, Propaganda and Total War*, 106.

10. Erinnerungen von Walter Koch (*1870) aus Dresden, Chef des Sächsischen Landeslebensmittelamtes, (DHM-Bestand), Lebendiges Leben Online, Deutsches Historisches Museum, accessed November 22, 2014, www.dhm.de/lemo/forum/kollektives_gedaechtnis/065/index.html.

11. Welch, *Germany, Propaganda and Total War*, 111.

12. Welch, *Germany, Propaganda and Total War*, 119.

13. Welch, *Germany, Propaganda and Total War*, 120.

14. Welch, *Germany, Propaganda and Total War*, 106. During the Nazi era, the recollection of this "pig murder" (*Schweinemord*) would often be employed as a dire warning of a misguided food policy.

15. See table in Welch, *Germany, Propaganda and Total War*, 125.

16. Welch, *Germany, Propaganda and Total War*, 125.

17. Welch, *Germany, Propaganda and Total War*, 127.

18. Welch, *Germany, Propaganda and Total War*, 117.

19. Nellie De Lissa, "War-Rime Cookery" (Simpkon and Marshall, 1915), 5–7. Reprinted in *World War I and European Society: A Sourcebook*, eds. Marilyn Shevin-Coetzee and Franz Coetzee (Lexington: D.C. Heath and Company, 1995), 148.

20. De Lissa, "War-Rime Cookery."

21. De Lissa, "War-Rime Cookery," 147.

22. De Lissa, "War-Rime Cookery," 147–48.

23. Peter Lummel, "Food Provisioning in the German Army of the First World War," in *Food and War in Twentieth Century Europe*, eds. Ina Zweiniger, Rachel Duffett, and Alain Drouard (Surrey, England: Ashgate, 2001), 13–25, 23.

24. Teuteberg, "Food Provisioning on the German Home Front," 59–72.

25. While the Nazis heavily exploited these feelings, the analysis of election data shows that the unemployed, for example, did not overproportionally vote for Hitler. See in more detail Jürgen W. Falter, *Hitler's Wähler* (Munich: Beck Verlag, 1991).

26. Alice Weinreb, "Matters of Taste: The Politics of Food and Hunger in Divided Germany, 1945–1971" (PhD dissertation, University of Michigan, 2009), 44.

27. See the exhibition catalog by Sonja Kinzler, *Kanonen statt Butter. Ernährung und Propaganda im "Dritten Reich"* (Kiel, 2006).

28. Weinreb, "Matters of Taste," 33ff.

29. Konrad Köstlin, "Der Eintopf der Deutschen. Das Zusammengekochte als Kultessen," in *Tübinger Beitrage zur Volkskultur*, eds. Utz Jeggle et al. (Tübingen: Gulde-Druck, 1986), 220–41.

30. Köstlin, "Der Eintopf der Deutschen," 235.

31. Weinreb, "Matters of Taste," 34.

32. Kinzler, *Kanonen statt Butter*, 17.

33. Here quoted from Weinreb, "Matters of Taste," 36.

34. Köstlin, "Der Eintopf der Deutschen," 235.

35. Anton Zischka, *Brot für zwei Milliarden Menschen* (Leipzig: W. Goldmann, 1938), 6–7, here quoted from Weinreb, "Matters of Taste," 40.

36. Horst Gies, "The NSDAP and Agrarian Organizations in the Final Phase of the Weimar Republic," in *Nazism and the Third Reich*, ed. H. A. Turner (New York: Quadrangle Books, 1972), 45–88.

37. On the development of Darré's ideology see Gesine Gerhard, "Breeding Pigs and People for the Third Reich: Richard Walter Darré's Agrarian Ideology," in *How Green Were the Nazis? Nature, Environment, and Nation in the Third Reich*, eds. Franz-Josef Brüggemeier, Mark Cioc, and Thomas Zeller (Athens: Ohio University Press, 2005), 129–46, 131f.

38. Richard Walther Darré, *Das Bauerntum als Lebensquell der nordischen Rasse*, 4th ed. (München: Lehmann, 1934), 26.

39. See Darré, *Das Bauerntum als Lebensquell* and the collection of his articles and speeches in Richard Walther Darré, *Um Blut und Boden. Reden und Aufsätze*, 4th ed. (München, 1942).

40. For an overview of agrarian romanticism see Klaus Bergmann, *Agrarromantik und Grosstadtfeindschaft* (Meisenheim a. Glan: Hain, 1970). See also Gesine Gerhard, "Bauernbewegung und Agrarromantik in der Weimarer Republik. Die Bauernhochschulbewegung und die Blut-und-Boden-Ideologie des Nationalsozialismus" (M.A. thesis, Technische Universität Berlin, 1994).

41. Ernst Moritz Arndt, "Über künftige ständische Verfassungen in Deutschland (1814)," in *Agrarpolitische Schriften*, ed. W. D. W. Terstegen (Goslar, 1938), 278, and Wilhelm Heinrich Riehl, *Die Naturgeschichte des deutschen*

Volkes als Grundlage einer deutschen Socialpolitik, 4 vols. (München, 1851–1869), 41.

42. See Darré's presentation on January 18, 1937, in which he explained the idea of blood. Document found in the city archives in Goslar (*Stadtarchiv Goslar*), personal collection Richard Walther Darré, vol. 431a, 2. For usage of the pair of words, see also: Mathias Eidenbenz, *"Blut und Boden": Zur Funktion und Genese der Metaphern des Agrarismus und Biologismus in der nationalsozialistischen Bauernpropaganda R. W. Darrés* (Bern: Peter Lang, 1993), 3–4.

43. So the title of Darré's book, *Das Bauerntum als Lebensquell der nordischen Rasse*.

44. See Richard Walther Darré, "Blut und Boden als Lebensgrundlagen der nordischen Rasse, 29.9.1933," in Darré, *Um Blut und Boden. Reden und Aufsätze*, 17–29, and other articles and speeches in Darré, *Um Blut und Boden*.

45. The title of one of his articles written in 1927 was "The Pig as Criterion for Nordic People and Semites" ("Das Schwein als Kriterium für Nordische Völker und Semiten").

46. Richard Walther Darré, "Das Zuchtziel des deutschen Volkes, 1931," in *Um Blut und Boden*, 30–40.

47. See Darré's written notes from a talk he gave on January 18, 1931. Document in Darré's personal collection in *Stadtarciv Goslar*, NL Darré, vol. 431a, fol. 6.

48. Hitler, here quoted from Weinreb, "Matters of Taste," 39.

49. Anna Bramwell interprets Darré's role differently. She states that the resettlement program was an "improvised response to a sudden emergency," and represented a "fusion of Darréan Blut und Boden ideology, demographic-national aims, and agrarian reform." Anna Bramwell, *Blood and Soil: Richard Walther Darré and Hitler's "Green Party"* (Abbotsbrook: Kensal Press, 1985), 169.

50. "Auf euren Schultern, Bauern und Landwirte, Landfrauen und Landarbeiter, ruht heute die doppelte Verantwortung. Setzt all eure Kräfte ein. Zeigt, was ihr zu leisten vermögt. Der Weg, der vor euch liegt, ist unendlich mühselig und schwer." Here quoted from Gustavo Corni and Horst Gies, *Brot—Butter—Kanonen. Die Ernährungswirtschaft in Deutschland unter der Diktatur Hitlers* (Berlin: Akademie Verlag, 1997), 406.

51. Here quoted from the Exhibition Catalogue of the Goslar Museum "Erntedank und Blut und Boden—Bückeberg/Hameln und Goslar 1933 bis 1938—NS-Rassekult und die Widerrede von Kirchengemeinden," ed. Verein Spurensuche Harzregione.V., 2010, 4.

52. Bernd Sösemann, *Appell unter der Erntekrone. Das Reichserntedankfest in der nationalsozialistischen Diktatur*, in: *Jahrbuch für Kommunikationsgeschichte* 2 (2000), S. 113–56, 116. The last time the Reichserntedankfest was held was in 1937. It was canceled just two days before the scheduled celebration

in 1938 because of the Czech crisis. After that, the war put an end to this kind of spectacle.

53. See Bernhard Gelderblom's website on the history of the city of Hameln, chapter "Bückeberg." Accessed November 22, 2014, www.gelderblom-hameln.de/bückeberg/bückeberg.html.

54. Gelderblom. Accessed on November 22, 2014, www.gelderblom-hameln.de/bückeberg/konzept/idee.html.

55. Sösemann, *Appell unter der Erntekrone*, 116.

56. See photos on Gelderblom's webpage, accessed November 22, 2014, www.gelderblom-hameln.de/bückeberg/baumassnahmen/grossbaustelle.html.

57. Sösemann, *Appell unter der Erntekrone*, 14.

58. See also Anke Sawahn, *Die Frauenlobby vom Land. Die Landfrauenbewegung in Deutschland und ihre Funktionärinnen 1898 bis 1948* (Frankfurt: DLG Verlag, 2009).

59. Sösemann, *Appell unter der Erntekrone*, 124.

60. Here quoted from Gelderblom, www.gelderblom-hameln.de/bückeberg/baumassnahmen/grossbaustelle.html.

61. Adam Tooze, *Wages of Destruction: The Making and Breaking of the German Nazi Economy* (New York: Penguin Books, 2008), 539.

2. EATING AT HOME

1. For a historical overview of food culture in Germany, see Ursula Heinzelmann, *Food Culture in Germany* (Westport, CT: Greenwood Press, 2008), 1–36.

2. Heinzelmann, *Food Culture in Germany*, 24.

3. Gustavo Corni and Horst Gies, *Brot—Butter—Kanonen. Die Ernährungswirtschaft in Deutschland unter der Diktatur Hitlers* (Berlin: Akademie Verlag, 1997), 44.

4. Corni and Gies, *Brot—Butter—Kanonen*, 24.

5. See, for example, J. Bergmann and K. Megerle, "Protest und Aufruhr der Landwirtschaft in der Weimarer Republik (1924–1933). Formen und Typen der politischen Agrarbewegung im regionalen Vergleich," in *Regionen im historischen Vergleich. Studien zu Deutschland im 19. und 20. Jahrhundert*, eds. J. Bergmann et al. (Opladen: Westdeutscher Verlag, 1989), 201–87. Regional case studies include R. Pomp, *Bauern und Grossgrundbesitzer auf ihrem Weg ins Dritte Reich. Der Brandenburgische Landbund, 1918–1933* (Berlin: Akademie Verlag, 2011), and G. Stoltenberg, *Politische Strömungen im deutschen Landvolk, 1918–1933. Ein Beitrag zur politischen Meinungsbildung in der Weimarer Republik* (Düsseldorf: Droste Verlag), 1962.

6. On the political takeover of agrarian interest groups and rural parties see Horst Gies, "The NSDAP and Agrarian Organizations in the Final Phase of the Weimar Republic," in *Nazism and the Third Reich*, ed. H. A. Turner (New York: Quadrangle Books, 1972), 45–88.

7. This assessment differs from earlier interpretations where historians concluded that "Nazi agricultural policies were successful in augmenting food production and increasing national self-sufficiency." Citation from Mark Spoerer and Jochen Streb, "Guns and Butter—But No Margarine: The Impact of Nazi Agricultural and Consumption Policies on German Food Production and Consumption, 1933–38" (paper prepared for the XIV International Economic History Congress, 2006), 3. See Spoerer and Streb, "Guns and Butter—But No Margarine," 3–5.

8. Spoerer and Streb, "Guns and Butter—But No Margarine," 6.

9. Jörg Baten and Andrea Wagner, "Autarchy, Market Disintegration, and Health: The Mortality and Nutritional Crisis in Nazi Germany, 1933–1937," *Economics and Human Biology* 1 (2002): 1–28.

10. Völkischer Beobachter, here quoted from Corinna Treitel, "Nature and the Nazi Diet," *Food and Foodways* 17 (2009): 139–58, 144.

11. Treitel, "Nature and the Nazi Diet," 146.

12. Lizzie Collingham, *The Taste of War: World War I and the Battle for Food* (New York: Penguin Press, 2012), 355.

13. Treitel, "Nature and the Nazi Diet."

14. Picker, Hitler's Tischgespräche, here quoted from Collingham, *The Taste of War*, 377.

15. Here quoted from Collingham, *The Taste of War*, 377.

16. Collingham, *The Taste of War*, 377.

17. Here quoted from Collingham, *The Taste of War*, 357.

18. Treitel, "Nature and the Nazi Diet," 146.

19. See chapter 5 on the relationship between the Nazis and organic farmers.

20. Stefano Grando and Gianluca Volpi, "Backwardness, Modernization, Propaganda: Agrarian Policies and Rural Representations in the Italian Fascist Regime," in *Agriculture in the Age of Fascism: Authoritarian Technocracy and Rural Modernization, 1922–1945*, eds. Lourenzo Fernández-Prieto, Juan Pan-Montojo, and Miguel Cabo (Turnboat, Belgium: Brepols, 2014), 43–84.

21. Corni and Gies, *Brot—Butter—Kanonen*, 261.

22. Corni and Gies, *Brot—Butter—Kanonen*, 263.

23. Corni and Gies, *Brot—Butter—Kanonen*, 308.

24. Corni and Gies, *Brot—Butter—Kanonen*, 315.

25. In 1934 it covered 80 percent, in 1935, 84 percent, and in 1936, 80 percent. Corni and Gies, *Brot—Butter—Kanonen*, 265–71.

26. Corni and Gies use slightly different numbers in their study. They state that the deficit in fat decreased from 62.8 percent in 1928 to 52.8 percent in 1938 (*Brot—Butter—Kanonen*, 311ff).

27. Corni and Gies, *Brot—Butter—Kanonen*, 273.

28. Corni and Gies, *Brot—Butter—Kanonen*, 273–74.

29. The rationing system had been designed by nutritionists from the Institute for the Physiology of Work under Heinrich Kraut. See also chapter 5.

30. Corni and Gies, *Brot—Butter—Kanonen*, 555.

31. Collingham, *The Taste of War*, 360.

32. Collingham, *The Taste of War*, 368.

33. Corni and Gies, *Brot—Butter—Kanonen*, 558.

34. Here quoted from Corni and Gies, *Brot—Butter—Kanonen*, 559.

35. Corni and Gies, *Brot—Butter—Kanonen*, 559.

36. Corni and Gies, *Brot—Butter—Kanonen*, 561.

37. Corni and Gies, *Brot—Butter—Kanonen*, 562–63.

38. On the conflict between Darré and Backe see Gesine Gerhard, "Food and Genocide. Nazi Agrarian Food Policy in the Occupied Territories of the Soviet Union," *Contemporary European History* 18, no. 1 (2009): 45–65.

39. Corni and Gies, *Brot—Butter—Kanonen*, 564.

40. On the connection between euthanasia and the Holocaust, see Henry Friedlander, *The Origins of Nazi Genocide: From Euthanasia to the Final Solution* (Chapel Hill: University of North Carolina Press, 1995).

41. See Robert Lifton, *The Nazi Doctors: Medical Killing and the Psychology of Genocide* (New York: Basic Books, 2000).

42. Collingham, *The Taste of War*, 360–61. See also Lifton, *The Nazi Doctors*, 429–30.

43. See Alice Weinreb, "Matters of Taste: the Politics of Food and Hunger in Divided Germany, 1945–1971" (PhD diss., University of Michigan, 2009).

44. Weinreb, "Matters of Taste," 60.

45. Collingham, *The Taste of War*, 160.

46. This contrast between the "better" treatment of forced laborers in the countryside and the harsh treatment in industry has recently been questioned. The range of personal behaviors and relationships between peasants and forced laborers has been more carefully examined by Ela Hornung, Enst Langthaler, and Sabine Schweitzer, "Forced Labor in Agriculture," in *German Wartime Society, 1939–1945*, ed. Jörg Echternkamp, *German Wartime Society, 1939–1945* (Oxford: Oxford University Press, 2014), 581–668.

47. Collingham, *The Taste of War*, 371.

48. Adam Tooze, *The Wages of Destruction: The Making and Breaking of the Nazi Economy* (New York: Penguin Books, 2007), 517.

49. More on the treatment of Soviet POWs in chapter 3.

50. See, for example, Susanne Heim, *Kalorien, Kautschuk, Karrieren. Pflanzenzüchtung und landwirtschaftliche Forschung in Kaiser-Wilhelm-Instituten, 1933–1945* (Göttingen: Wallstein Verlag, 2003). See chapter 5.

51. See chapter 5.

52. Here quoted from Collingham, *The Taste of War*, 372.

53. Jonathan North, "Soviet Prisoners of War: Forgotten Nazi Victims of World War II," *World War II Magazine*, January/February 2006. Here quoted from HistoryNet.com, accessed October 28, 2013, www.historynet.com/soviet-prisoners-of-war-forgotten-nazi-victims-of-world-war-ii.htm.

54. Tooze, *The Wages of Destruction*, 523.

55. Collingham, *The Taste of War*, 374–400.

56. Corni and Gies, *Brot—Butter—Kanonen*, 576.

57. "Es liegt auf der Hand, dass die ungünstigeren Faktoren die günstigen einer mittleren bis guten Ernte weit übersteigen." Here quoted from Corni and Gies, *Brot—Butter—Kanonen*, 576.

58. Corni and Gies, *Brot—Butter—Kanonen*, 577.

59. Corni and Gies, *Brot—Butter—Kanonen*, 581.

60. See chapter 6.

61. Heinzelmann, *Food Culture in Germany*, 37. See chapter 6.

62. See, for example, Arnd Bauernkämper, "Agrarwirtschaft und ländliche Gesellschaft in der Bundesrepublik Deutschland und der DDR. Eine Bilanz der Jahre, 1945–1965," *Aus Politik und Zeitgeschichte* B 38/97 (1997): 25–37. See also Antonia Humm, *Auf dem Weg zum sozialistischen Dorf? Zum Wandel der dörflichen Lebenswelt in der DDR und der Bundesrepublik Deutschland, 1952–1969* (Göttingen: Vandenhoeck & Ruprecht, 1999).

63. Corni and Gies, *Brot—Butter—Kanonen*, 582.

64. Here quoted from Corni and Gies, *Brot—Butter—Kanonen*, 579.

65. Here quoted from Corni and Gies, *Brot—Butter—Kanonen*, 581.

66. Arnulf Hügel, *Kriegsernährungswirtschaft Deutschlands während des Ersten und Zweiten Weltkriegs* (Konstanz: Hartung-Gorre-Verlag, 2003), 445–54.

67. Corni and Gies, *Brot—Butter—Kanonen*, 573.

3. HERBERT BACKE AT THE CENTER OF FOOD POLITICS

1. Gesine Gerhard, "Food and Genocide: Nazi Agrarian Food Policy in the Occupied Territories of the Soviet Union," *Contemporary European History* 18, no. 1 (2009): 45–65.

2. I would like to thank Armgard Backe for allowing me to make a photocopy of the document in her possession, "Aufzeichnungen von Hortense Backe"

(Recollections of Hortense Backe), dated 1968. Her brother took me to the copy center in town after my visit.

3. "Aufzeichnungen von Hortense Backe."

4. See Bernd Alleweldt, *Herbert Backe—Eine politische Biographie* (MA thesis, Goethe Universität Frankfurt, 2000), 10.

5. "Aufzeichnungen von Hortense Backe."

6. Information provided by Armgard Henning, née Backe, February 4, 2008.

7. Here quoted from Joachim Lehmann, "Herbert Backe—Technokrat und Agrarideologe," in *Die Braune Elite II. 21 Weitere Biographische Skizzen*, edited by Ronald Smelzer, Enrico Syring and Rainer Zitelmann (Darmstadt: Wissenschaftliche Buchgesellschaft, 1993), 1–12.

8. See Herbert Backe, *Um die Nahrungsfreiheit Europas. Weltwirtschaft oder Großraum*, 2nd ed. (Leipzig: Wilhelm Goldmann Verlag, 1943). See also Adam Tooze, *The Wages of Destruction: The Making and Breaking of the Nazi Economy*, 174, and Ernst Langthaler, "Agrar-Europa unter Nationalsozialistischen Vorzeichen (1933–1945)," in *Themenportal Europäische Geschichte*, www.euopa.clio-online.de, June 19, 2011.

9. See table in Tooze, *Wages of Destruction*, 176.

10. Tooze, *Wages of Destruction*, 176–77.

11. Tooze, *Wages of Destruction*, 180.

12. Backe wrote his own sort of political testament while awaiting his trial in the Nuremberg prison and called it *Grosser Bericht* or "Great Report." See the collection of Backe's personal papers (*Nachlaß*) in the German Federal Archive in Koblenz (*Bundesarchiv*), referenced here as "Grosser Bericht," BAK NL Backe, 3.

13. Backe finished his thesis on the Russian grain market, but it was not accepted by the University's dissertation committee and he was never awarded a doctoral degree. The dissertation was later reprinted and circulated among Nazi leaders and informed the economic planning for Operation Barbarossa.

14. Backe and his wife exchanged long and frequent letters while he was in Berlin and his family in Hornsen. These letters are among Backe's personal papers in the Federal Archives in Koblenz. The Hornsen farm would also secure financial support for the family after the death of their father in 1948. When the lease ended in 1949, Ursula negotiated successfully for compensation for the farm inventory that was the property of the family. Conversation with Backe family in Hanover in 2007.

15. Gerhard, "Food and Genocide," 49f.

16. Alleweldt, *Herbert Backe*, 12. Backe's party number was 22,766.

17. For his critique of liberalism, see Herbert Backe, *Um die Nahrungsfreiheit Europas. Weltwirtschaft oder Großraum*, 2nd ed. (Leipzig: Wilhelm Goldmann Verlag, 1943), and *Volk und Wirtschaft im national-sozialistischen Deutschland.*

Reden des Staatssekretärs im Reichs- und Preussischen Ministerium für Ernährung und Landwirtschaft (Berlin: Reichsnährstandsverlag, o.J.).

18. Here quoted from Lehmann, "Herbert Backe—Technokrat und Agrarideologe." 4.

19. Backe, *Grosser Bericht*, 7.

20. See Backe, *Grosser Bericht*, 8.

21. Letter to Ursula Backe from March 21, 1933, in BAK NL Backe, no. 1.

22. Letter to Ursula from April 8, 1941, BAK NL Backe, no. 1. This and many other letters, as well as Ursula Backe's diaries and the aforementioned *Grosser Bericht* can all be found in the personal collection of Herbert Backe in the Federal Archives in Koblenz, signature BAK NL 1075. Hereafter cited as, BAK NL Backe.

23. Backe, *Grosser Bericht*, 8. See also Gerhard, "Food and Genocide," 49–50.

24. Here quoted from Joachim Fest, *Speer: The Final Verdict* (New York: Harcourt, 2001), 29.

25. Backe, *Grosser Bericht*, 12.

26. Backe, *Grosser Bericht*, 10–12.

27. See Ursula's diary entries from June 27, 1933, May 5, 1934, February 4, 1935, and December 18, 1934, BA NL Backe, no. 18. Ursula Backe's diaries form an important part of this study of Backe's ideology and politics. In her diary entries, she wrote little about her own personal feelings or her children. For more than twenty years, she wrote about her husband's political convictions and daily struggles with a clear conscience that "great things were happening" that needed to be recorded for posterity. See also the introductory chapter.

28. One of Albrecht's middle names is accordingly "Walther." From my conversation with the Backe siblings on June 2, 2004, and a personal letter from Albrecht Backe dated September 2, 2004. See also Ursula Backe's diary entry from May 5, 1934, describing the baptism.

29. The original copy of Ursula Backe's diary (six volumes) is in the Federal Archives in Koblenz, Germany.

30. Backe, Diary entry April 22, 1934.

31. Backe, Diary entry May 5, 1934.

32. See letters from November 23, 1944, February 4, 1945, and August 2, 1943, BAK NL Backe, no. 1. See also Ursula Backe's diary entry on August 7, 1944, BAK NL Backe, no. 19.

33. Two conversations with the Backe children in their hometown of Hanover in 2004 and again in 2007 added further valuable information that I would not have been able to find in any archive. I am especially grateful to Albrecht Backe, who arranged these meetings and who responded to my e-mails and phone calls. As described in the introductory chapter, the personal contact opened another

line of exploration. I wondered how the Backe family lived with the legacy of their father (or husband) as a Nazi perpetrator. For a historian researching the murderous policies of a perpetrator, the conversations with the family were both a blessing and a hindrance. It allowed me to understand (and gain access) to a man whom I would otherwise just have known from written comments. It also created a dilemma for me, because the children made it clear that they didn't want a historian to use the documents to besmirch their father's memory. When I worked with the sources, however, Backe's responsibility became quite clear. He was in charge of food rations for Germany, the occupied territories in the East, and for Soviet POWs. Reading Backe's words and his disregard for the lives of Soviet citizens he considered to be useless eaters, naturally did not endear the man to me. But historians have long learned that Nazi perpetrators were not just merciless monsters. Many of them were loving family fathers and husbands, who wrote sentimental letters while their murderous policies were executed. It is more important to understand what motivated them and how they came to make the decisions they did.

34. Gesine Gerhard, "Breeding Pigs and People for the Third Reich: Richard Walter Darré's Agrarian Ideology," in *How Green Were the Nazis? Nature, Environment, and Nation in the Third Reich*, ed. by Franz-Josef Brüggemeier, Marc Cioc, and Thomas Zeller (Athens: Ohio University Press, 2005), 132–35; Gesine Gerhard, "Food as a Weapon: Agricultural Sciences and the Building of a Greater German Empire," *Food, Culture and Society* 14, no. 3 (2011): 337–40.

35. Darré described this meeting at the architect Paul Schultze-Naumburg's residence in Saaleck in a letter to his friend Georg Kenstler, the Artaman League leader. According to Darré, Hitler thought that he had not emphasized the "Jewish problem" enough in his writings. See Darré's letter to Kenstler from April 25, 1930, in city archives in Goslar, personal collection Richard Walther Darré, vol. 94. Anna Bramwell used this alleged lack of anti-Semitism in Darré's work as an argument to support her claim that Darré did not go along with the Nazis' racial extermination policies. However, Darré himself said that Hitler was not well informed about his writings. In fact, Darré's early writings are clearly anti-Semitic. See Anna Bramwell, *Blood and Soil: Richard Walther Darré and Hitler's "Green Party"* (Abbotsbrook: Kensal Press, 1985). See also Gesine Gerhard, "Richard Walther Darré—Naturschützer oder 'Rassenzüchter'?" in Joachim Radkau and Frank Uekötter (eds.), *Naturschutz und Nationalsozialismus* (Frankfurt/New York: Campus Verlag, 2003), 257–72.

36. The SS marriage order required SS men to apply for a permit to get married. The spouse's racial "purity" was to be checked to ensure the "upbreeding" of the SS.

37. See also Tooze, *Wages of Destruction*, 171, and Richard Breitmann, *The Architect of Genocide: Himmler and the Final Solution* (New York: Knopf, 1991).

38. By 1932, the agricultural interest organizations had been infiltrated and the most important agrarian party, the Christian National Peasants' and Rural People's Party had lost all its seats in the parliament. See Larry Eugene Jones, "Crisis and Realignment: Agrarian Splinter Parties in the Late Weimar Republic, 1928–1933," in *Peasants and Lords in Modern Germany: Recent Studies in Agricultural History*, ed. Robert G. Moeller (Boston: Allen & Unwin, 1986), 198–232; Horst Gies, "The NSDAP and Agrarian Organizations in the Final Phase of the Weimar Republic," in *Nazism and the Third Reich*, ed. Henry A. Turner (New York: Quadrangle Books, 1972), 45–88, and Horst Gies, "Die nationalsozialistische Machtergreifung auf dem agrarpolitischen Sektor," *Zeitschrift für Agrargeschichte und Agrarsoziologie*, vol. 16 (1967): 210–32.

39. John E. Farquharson, "The Agrarian Policy of National Socialist Germany," in *Peasants and Lords in Modern Germany: Recent Studies in Agricultural History*, ed. Robert G. Moeller (Boston: Allen & Unwin, 1986), 233–59.

40. "Der nationalsozialistische landwirtschaftliche Fachbearbeiter." Here quoted from Gies, "The NSDAP and Agrarian Organizations," 51.

41. The *Nationalsozialistische Landpost* was first published in September 1931.

42. Gustavo Corni, *Hitler and the Peasants: Agrarian Policy of the Third Reich, 1930–1939* (New York: Berg, 1990), 66–115.

43. See Corni, *Hitler and the Peasants*, 66–86.

44. See Bramwell, *Blood and Soil*, 109; and Corni, *Hitler and the Peasants*, 80–81.

45. In his own defense during the Nuremberg trials in 1949 Darré argued before the military tribunal that the autonomy of the RNS and the hostility of other organizations toward the RNS was yet more proof of his departure from the official Nazi line. See Darré's defense, BAK NL Darré 1094 I, no. 1, folio 9–17.

46. Corni, *Hitler and the Peasants*, 74.

47. See, for example, Darré's letter to Göring from November 1, 1936. Darré wrote this letter while recuperating from a long illness. SA Goslar, NL Darré, vol. 146.

48. Heirs had to prove their non-Jewish ancestry back to 1800.

49. The law of hereditary entailment was issued on September 29, 1933. On the law see especially Friedrich Grundmann, *Agrarpolitik im 3. Reich. Anspruch und Wirklichkeit des Reichserbhofgesetzes* (Hamburg: Hoffmann und Campe, 1979).

50. Corni, *Hitler and the Peasants*, 144.

51. Corni, *Hitler and the Peasants*, 145–48.

52. Corni, *Hitler and the Peasants*, 146–48. See also Tooze, *Wages of Destruction*, 182–86.

53. As Ernst Langthaler pointed out, it was not just the Erbhof Law itself that encountered hostility. Peasants used the special courts to dispute family members' claims or to litigate other family conflicts over questions of inheritance. See Ernst Langthaler, "From Capitalism to 'Neo-Feudalism'? Property Relations, Land Markets and the Nazi State in the German Province of Niederdonau, 1938–1945," in *Contexts of Property in Europe. The Social Embeddedness of Property Rights in Land in Historical Perspective* (Rural History in Europe 5), eds. Rosa Congost and Rui Santos (Brepols: Turnhout 2010), 165–86.

54. Corni, *Hitler and the Peasants*, 151; Tooze, *Wages of Destruction*, 186.

55. See Darré's letter to Backe from December 27, 1934, BAK NL Backe, no. 10. See also Darré's personal dedication in BAK NL Backe, no. 1 and Ursula Backe's diary entry on May 5, 1934, BAK NL Backe, no. 17.

56. Letter to Ursula from October 14, 1933, BAK NL Backe, no. 1. See also Backe's letter dated September 30, 1933, BAK NL Backe 1075, no. 1.

57. Corni and Gies, *Brot—Butter—Kanonen,* 420–21; and Corni, *Hitler and the Peasants*, 145–48. See also Gesine Gerhard, "Breeding Pigs and People for the Third Reich: Richard Walter Darré's Agrarian Ideology," in *How Green Were the Nazis? Nature, Environment, and Nation in the Third Reich*, eds. Franz-Josef Brüggemeier, Mark Cioc, and Thomas Zeller (Athens: Ohio University Press, 2005), 129–46, 135.

58. Backe, *Grosser Bericht*, 18.

59. For a detailed analysis of the relationship between Backe and Darré, see Gerhard, "Food and Genocide," 51–54.

60. See, for example, the entry on October 15, 1934, BAK NL Backe, no. 17. See also Backe's letters to Ursula dated September 6, 1933, June 16, 1935, and September 4, 1936, BAK NL Backe, no. 1.

61. Letter to Ursula dated September 6, 1933, BAK NL Backe, no. 1.

62. Letters to his wife from May 3, 1932 [probably 1933], and May 4, 1933, BAK NL Backe, no. 1.

63. See Herbert's letter to his wife Ursula from September 6, 1933, BAK NL Backe, no. 1. Backe believed Darré would make an excellent foreign minister. Letters to his wife dated June 9, 1933, BAK NL Backe, no. 1

64. Letter to Ursula from July 5, 1935, BAK NL Backe, no. 1.

65. Letter to Ursula from September 4, 1936, BAK NL Backe, no. 1. See also Backe, *Grosser Bericht*, 21.

66. Letter to Ursula from July 5, 1935, BAK NL Backe, no. 1. See also the letter from August 20, 1936, BAK NL Backe, no. 1. At this point in time, however, he also showed loyalty to his boss. See his letter to Ursula dated July 24, 1937, BAK NL Backe, no. 1.

67. Darré's diary entry on March 2, 1936. Darré's diaries were edited after the war by a friend and can only be used with great caution. A copy of the edited diaries is in the Stadtarchiv Goslar (SA) NL Darré, no. 484n and in BAK NL Darré I, no. 65a.

68. This apologetic account of Darré's role can also be found in Bramwell.

69. Ursula Backe's diary entry on May 30, 1941, BAK NL Backe, no. 20.

70. Letter to Ursula Backe July 1, 1934.

71. Diary entry on May 5, 1934.

72. Soon after his appointment, Göring assured Backe that he was "more than a minister." Ursula Backe's diary entry on October 23, 1936, BAK NL Backe, no. 19.

73. Diary entries on November 8 and 25, 1936, BAK NL Backe, no. 19.

74. Darré's letter from December 9, 1939, BAK R 43 II, no. 356b, fol. 17.

75. Letter from December 11, 1939, BAK R 43 II, no. 356b. See also Darré's diary entry on February 5, 1937, BAK N 1094 I, no. 65a.

76. Darré's letter from August 25, 1941, BAK N 1094 II, no. 20.

77. Darré's letter to Backe from March 14, 1941, BAK NL Backe, no. 10. See also Darré's diary entry on March 14, 1941, SAG N Darré, no. 484.

78. Darré's letter to Backe from March 14, 1941, BAK NL Backe, no. 10. We cannot be sure that these comments (in red marker) were made by Backe. However, given the fact that the letter was in a folder with other personal letters written by Backe to his wife, it is very likely that these are his comments. See his letter to his wife dated April 8, 1941, BAK NL Backe, no. 1.

79. Backe's letter to his wife from April 8, 1941, BAK NL Backe, no. 1.

80. Ursula Backe's diary entry from July 26, 1941, BAK NL Backe, no. 20. Again in April 1942, Backe explained that he could not work any longer with Darré and asked Martin Bormann to make a decision. Diary entry on April 11, 1942 and April 17, 1942, BAK NL Backe, no. 20. In May 1942, Backe asked Hitler directly to give him full responsibility. See the diary entry on May 10, 1942, BAK NL Backe, no. 20.

81. See memos from May 1942 in BAK R 43 II, no. 1143. See also Ursula's diary entry on May 13, 1942, BAK NL Backe, no. 20.

4. THE *HUNGERPLAN*

1. Here Wolfgang Benz, *Hans-Joachim Riecke, NS-Staatsekretär. Vom Hungerplaner vor, zum "Welternährer" nach 1945* (Berlin: Wissenschaftlicher Verlag Berlin, 2014), 54–55.

2. Hitler on August 11, 1939, here quoted from Alex J. Kay, *Exploitation, Resettlement, Mass Murder: Political and Economic Planning for German Oc-*

cupation Policy in the Soviet Union, 1940–1941 (New York/Oxford: Berghahn Books, 2006), 40. See also Gesine Gerhard, "Food and Genocide: Nazi Agrarian Food Policy in the Occupied Territories of the Soviet Union," *Contemporary European History* 18, no. 1 (2009): 45–65, 56.

3. Here quoted from Timothy Snyder, *Bloodlands: Europe between Hitler and Stalin* (New York: Basic Books, 2010), 159. Compared to other industrialized countries, Germany had only 2.1 hectares of arable land per farmer. See table in Tooze, *Wages of Destruction*, 176.

4. Here quoted from Gustavo Corni and Horst Gies, *Brot—Butter—Kanonen. Die Ernährungswirtschaft in Deutschland unter der Diktatur Hitlers* (Berlin: Akademie Verlag, 1997), 451. See also Gerhard, "Food and Genocide," 56.

5. Kay, *Exploitation*, 36. Riecke had worked for Backe in the Reich Ministry since 1936 and had an "excellent" relationship with his boss. See Benz, *Riecke*, 32.

6. See the exchange of letters and memos between Backe, Darré, and Moritz in the German Federal Archive in Koblenz (*Bundesarchiv*) R 3601, fol. 7–28. See also Kay, *Exploitation*, 48; Wigbert Benz, *Der Hungerplan im "Unternehmen Barbarossa," 1941* (Berlin: Wissenschaftlicher Verlag, 2011), 32; Gerlach, *Kalkulierte Morde*, 71.

7. Introduction to the 1941 publication of Backe's *Die russische Getreidewirtschaft als Grundlage der Land- und Volkswirtschaft Rußlands*, I–IV.

8. Herbert Backe, *Um die Nahrungsfreiheit in Europa. Weltwirtschaft oder Grossraum*, 2nd ed. (Leipzig: Wilhelm Goldmann Verlag, 1942).

9. Backe, *Nahrungsfreiheit*, 500, 33.

10. See Kay, *Exploitation.*

11. Letter from Herbert Backe to his wife, April 8, 1941, BAK N 1975, no. 1. See also Gerhard, "Food and Genocide," 57.

12. The meeting included Backe's right-hand man in the Reich Ministry, Hans-Joachim Riecke. Benz, *Riecke*, 41. Summary notes from the meeting exist, but the notes do not include an exact list of attendees. See "Aktennotiz über die Besprechung der Staatssekretäre am 2.5.1941." Partially reprinted in Reinhard Rürup, ed., *Der Krieg gegen die Sowjetunion, 1941–1945. Eine Dokumentation* (Berlin: Argon Verlag, 1991), 44. See Alex J. Kay, "Germany's Staatssekretäre, Mass Starvation and the Meeting of May 2, 1941, " *Journal of Contemporary History* 41, no. 4 (2006), 685–700, and Kay, *Exploitation*, 125–26.

13. Here quoted from Benz, *Riecke*, 42.

14. "Aktennotiz." See reprint of document and Benz's comments on www.1000dokumente.de/index.html?c=dokument_de&dokument=0227_hun&object=facsimile&pimage=01&v=100&nav=&l=de.

15. See Kay, *Germany's Staatsekretäre.*

16. "Aktennotiz," partially reprinted in Rürup, *Der Krieg gegen die Sowjetunion*, 44.

17. Here quoted from Tooze, *Wages of Destruction*, 479.

18. Tooze, *Wages of Destruction*, 479–80.

19. "Wirtschaftspolitische Richtlinien des Wirtschaftsstabes Ost, Gruppe Landwirtschaft." Partially reprinted in Rürup, *Der Krieg*, 45.

20. *Wirtschaftspolitische Richtlinien*, here quoted from Benz, *Hungerplan*, 34.

21. Here quoted from Kay, *Exploitation*, 134.

22. Herbert Backe, *12 Gebote für das Verhalten der Deutschen im Osten und die Behandlung der Russen*, June 1, 1941. Reprinted in Rürup, *Der Krieg*, 46. Here quoted from Kay, *Exploitation*, 167.

23. Backe, *12 Gebote.*

24. See Gerhard, "Food and Genocide," and Kay, *Exploitation*. See also Götz Aly and Susanne Heim, *Vordenker der Vernichtung. Auschwitz und die deutschen Pläne für eine neue europäische Ordnung*, 2nd ed. (Frankfurt: Fischer Taschenbuch Verlag, 1993), Christian Gerlach, *Krieg, Ernährung, Völkermord. Deutsche Vernichtungspolitik im Zweiten Weltkrieg* (Zürich: Pendo Verlag, 2001).

25. Backe committed suicide in his prison cell about one week after the prosecutors questioned him about his authorship of the hunger plan. See the protocol of Kempner's interrogation of Backe on March 31, 1947, in BAK N 1470, no. 523.

26. See Ursula Backe's diary entries on September 22 and November 5, 1941, and the numerous entries in May 1942, BAK NL Backe, no. 20. See also Herbert Backe's letters to Ursula from August 18, 1942, and August 21, 1942, in BAK NL Backe, no. 1.

27. Hans Lammers and Martin Bormann were heads of the Nazi Party Chancellery, and Wilhelm Keitel was chief of the Wehrmacht.

28. Ursula Backe's diary entry on May 30, 1941, BAK NL Backe, no. 20. See also Gerhard, "Food and Genocide," 57.

29. Kay, *Exploitation*, 164–67.

30. Here quoted from Benz, *Riecke*, 43.

31. See also Rolf-Dieter Müller, "Die Konsequenzen der 'Volksgemeinschaft': Ernährung, Ausbeutung und Vernichtung," in *Der Zweite Weltkrieg. Analysen—Grundzüge—Forschungsbilanz*, ed. Wolfgang Michalka (Weyarn: Seehamer Verlag, 1989, 1997), 240–49, 244.

32. Here quoted from Benz, *Riecke*, 45.

33. Benz, *Riecke*, 45.

34. Gerlach, *Kalkulierte Morde*, 263.

35. Gerlach, *Kalkulierte Morde*, 257.

36. Benz, *Hungerplan*, 65.

37. Here quoted from Benz, *Riecke*, 47.

38. Tooze, *Wages of Destruction*, 485.

39. Here quoted from Snyder, *Bloodlands*, 175; Benz, *Hungerplan*, 68.

40. See K. C. Berkhoff, *Harvest of Despair: Life and Death in Ukraine under Nazi Rule* (Cambridge, MA: Belknap Press of Harvard University Press, 2004), 164–86.

41. Benz, *Hungerplan*, 71.

42. See the edited volume by Ulrich Herbert, *Europa und der "Reichseinsatz." Ausländische Zivilarbeiter, Kriegsgefangene und KZ-Häftlinge in Deutschland, 1938–1945* (Essen: Klartext Verlag, 1991).

43. Here quoted in Tooze, *Wages of Destruction*, 546.

44. Diary entry July 1941, BAK NL Backe, no. 20. See Gerhard, "Food and Genocide," 58.

45. Tooze, *Wages of Destruction*, 545, originally Gerlach, *Krieg Ernährung Völkermord*, 175.

46. Tooze, *Wages of Destruction*, 548–49.

47. Snyder, *Bloodlands*, 175.

48. Christian Streit, *Keine Kameraden. Die Wehrmacht und die sowjetischen Kriegsgefangenen, 1941–1945* (Stuttgart: Deutsche Verlagsanstalt, 1978), 128. Streit's book remains the authoritative study of the fate of Soviet POWs even forty years after its first publication.

49. Streit, *Keine Kameraden*, 8–10.

50. Streit, *Keine Kameraden*, 181.

51. See also Berkhoff, *Harvest of Despair*, 90.

52. For years, there were no studies of the fate of Soviet POWs in historical literature. The first studies came from outside Germany (Alexander Dallin in 1957, and the Polish researcher Szymon Daltner in 1964). Interest in the topic started to grow only in the 1960s. Christian Streit's *Keine Kameraden* was the first major work on the topic to appear in German in 1978. Streit was the first to implicate the culpability of the German Army. Republished in 1991, Streit's book is still the most comprehensive and authoritative work on the subject.

53. Berkhoff, *Harvest of Despair*, 92.

54. Berkhoff, *Harvest of Despair*, 92.

55. Streit, *Keine Kameraden*, 79.

56. Streit, *Keine Kameraden*, 128.

57. Streit, *Keine Kameraden*, 79.

58. Streit, *Keine Kameraden*, 141–42.

59. Here quoted from Streit, *Keine Kameraden*, 142.

60. Streit, *Keine Kameraden*, 143.

61. See chapter 5.

62. Quoted from Streit *Keine Kameraden*, 145. See Gerhard, "Food and Genocide," 62.
63. Streit *Keine Kameraden*, 145.
64. Streit, *Keine Kameraden*, 146–47.
65. Streit, *Keine Kameraden*, 162–71.
66. Gerlach, *Kalkulierte Morde*, 785.
67. Snyder, *Bloodlands*, 168.
68. Benz, *Hungerplan*, 75.

5. THE SCIENCE OF FOOD

1. See Gesine Gerhard, "Food as a Weapon. Agricultural Sciences and the Building of a Greater German Empire," *Food, Culture and Society* 14, no. 3 (2011): 335–51.
2. Susanne Heim, Carola Sachse, and Mark Walker, eds., *The Kaiser Wilhelm Society under National Socialism* (New York: Cambridge University Press, 2009).
3. The history of the sciences under the Nazis has only recently become the topic of closer scrutiny. Newer studies have emphasized that the Nazi State made great use of modern science and utilized it to promote its goals. The first critical examination of two Kaiser Wilhelm institutes and their "murderous" crimes was the study by Benno Müller-Hill, *Murderous Science: Elimination by Scientific Selection of Jews, Gypsies, and Others in Germany, 1933–1945* (New York: Oxford University Press, 1988). See also Margit Szöllösi-Janze, "National Socialism and the Sciences: Reflections, Conclusions and Historical Perspectives," in *Science in the Third Reich*, ed. Margit Szöllösi-Janze (Oxford: Berg, 2001), 1–36. See also the book series edited by Reinhard Rürup and Wolfgang Schieder, *Geschichte der Kaiser-Wilhelm-Gesellschaft im Nationalsozialismus*, 17 vols. (Göttingen: Wallstein Verlag, 2000–2007), and the book series edited by Rüdiger vom Bruch, Ulrich Herbert, and Patrick Wagner, *Studien zur Geschichte der Deutschen Forschungsgemeinschaft*, 5 vols. (Stuttgart: Steiner Verlag, 2007–2010).
4. See, for example, the collected essays in Susanne Heim, ed., *Autarkie und Ostexpansion. Pflanzenzucht und Agrarforschung im Nationalsozialismus* (Göttingen: Wallstein Verlag, 2002), and Hans-Walter Schmuhl, "Rasse, Rassenforschung, Rassenpolitik. Annäherung an das Thema, " in *Rassenforschung an Kaiser-Wilhelm-Instituten vor und nach 1933*, ed. Hans-Walter Schmuhl (Göttingen: Wallstein Verlag, 2003). See also Bernd Gausemeier, *Natürliche Ordnungen und politische Allianzen. Biologische und biochemische Forschung an Kaiser-Wilhelm-Instituten, 1933–1945* (Göttingen: Wallstein Verlag, 2005).

5. Dietrich Eichholtz, "Die 'Krautaktion.' Ruhrindustrie, Ernährungswissenschaft und Zwangsarbeit, 1944," in Ulrich Herbert (ed.) *Europa und der 'Reichseinsatz.' Ausländische Zivilarbeiter, Kriegsgefangene und KZ-Häftlinge in Deutschland, 1938–1945* (Essen: Klartext Verlag, 1991), 270–94, 281; Anna Zięba, "Das Nebenlager Rajsko," *Hefte von Auschwitz* 9 (1966): 75–108, 91.

6. Gausemeier, *Natürliche Ordnungen*, and Ute Deichmann, *Biologen unter Hitler. Porträt einer Wissenschaft im NS-Staat* (Frankfurt: Fischer Taschenbuch Verlag, 1995), 174.

7. Carola Sachse, ed., *Die Verbindung nach Auschwitz. Biowissenschaften und Menschenversuche an Kaiser-Wilhelm-Instituten. Dokumentation eines Symposiums* (Göttingen: Wallstein Verlag, 2003).

8. See, for example, Uwe Hossfeld and Carl-Gustaf Thornström, "'Rasches Zupacken.' Heinz Brücher und das botanische Sammelkommando der SS nach Rußland 1943," in Heim, *Autarkie und Ostexpansion*, 119–44.

9. Between 1933 and 1944 the revenues of the KWS almost tripled. See Rüdiger Hachtmann, "A Success Story? Highlighting the History of the Kaiser Wilhelm Society's General Administration in the Third Reich," in *The Kaiser Wilhelm Society under National Socialism*, eds. Susanne Heim, Carola Sachse, and Mark Walker (New York: Cambridge University Press, 2009), 19–46, 23.

10. On the history of the Reich Research Council, see Sören Flachowsky, *Von der Notgemeinschaft zum Reichsforschungsrat: Wissenschaftspolitik im Kontext von Autarkie, Aufrüstung, und Krieg* (Stuttgart: Franz Steiner, 2008).

11. Gerhard, *Food as a Weapon*, 343.

12. Susanne Heim, *Kalorien, Kautschuk, Karrieren. Pflanzenzüchtung und Landwirtschaftliche Forschung in Kaiser-Wilhelm-Instituten, 1933–1945* (Göttingen: Wallstein Verlag, 2003), 52.

13. Heim, *Kalorien*, 33.

14. Kristie Macrakis, *Surviving the Swastika: Scientific Research in Nazi Germany* (New York: Oxford University Press, 1993), 178.

15. See Gerhard, *Food as a Weapon.* Here quoted from Heim, *Forschung für die Autarkie*, 159.

16. The three new institutes were the Institute for the Science of Agricultural Work in Breslau, the Institute for Agricultural Science in Sofia, and the Institute for Cultivated Plant Research near Vienna. See Macrakis, *Surviving the Swastika*, 143, and Gerhard, *Food as a Weapon.*

17. Macrakis, *Surviving the Swastika*, 141–43. See also Heim, *Kalorien*, 92–93.

18. Rudolf Mentzel, Undersecretary in the Reich Ministry of Education (REM), sat on the advising board of the KWS and was the society's second vice president from 1940 to 1944. He was also president of the DFG (*Deutsche*

Forschungsgemeinschaft) from 1937 to 1939. Here quoted from Deichmann, *Biologen unter Hitler*, 174.

19. Here quoted from Heim, *Kalorien*, 40.

20. Susanne Heim, "Kog-Sagyz—A Vital War Reserve," in Heim, Sachse, and Walker, *The Kaiser Wilhelm Society*, 173–99.

21. Thomas Wieland, "Die politischen Aufgaben der deutschen Pflanzenzüchtung. NS-Ideologie und die Forschungsarbeiten der akademischen Pflanzenzüchter," in Heim, *Autarkie und Ostexpansion*, 35–56, 50.

22. Heinrich Kraut had joined the NSDAP in 1937, was a consultant to the Ministry of Food, and was a member of the Rationing Committee. His personal papers are in the Bundesarchiv in Koblenz, Germany. The Institute for Labor Physiology had been founded in 1912 in Berlin as one of the first institutes under the Kaiser Wilhelm Society. The institute relocated to Dortmund in the Ruhr area in 1926. It included divisions for labor psychology, physiology, chemistry, and nutrition. Jennifer Alexander, "An Efficiency of Scarcity: Using Food to Increase the Productivity of Soviet Prisoners of War in the Mines of the Third Reich," *History and Technology* 4, 22 (2006): 391–406, 396. See also Dietrich Eichholtz, "Die 'Krautaktion.' Ruhrindustrie, Ernährungswissenschaft und Zwangsarbeit 1944," in *Europa und der "Reichseinsatz." Ausländische Zivilarbeiter, Kriegsgefangene und KZ-Häftlinge in Deutschland, 1938–1945*, eds. Ulrich Herbert (Essen: Klartext Verlag, 1991), 270–94.

23. Alexander, "An Efficiency of Scarcity," 394.

24. See also chapter 2.

25. Alexander, "An Efficiency of Scarcity," 402.

26. Ulrich Herbert, ed., *Europa und der "Reichseinsatz." Ausländische Zivilarbeiter, Kriegsgefangene und KZ-Häftlinge in Deutschland, 1938–1945* (Essen: Klartext Verlag, 1991). See also chapter 4.

27. During the world wars, the term "Kraut" was used in English as a derogatory nickname for a German.

28. Alexander, "An Efficiency of Scarcity," 397.

29. Alexander, "An Efficiency of Scarcity," 399–400.

30. Alexander, "An Efficiency of Scarcity," 396.

31. See Eichholtz, "Die 'Krautaktion,'" 281.

32. See Eichholtz, "Die 'Krautaktion,'" 270–94. See also Heim, *Kalorien*, 107–20.

33. Kraut published his finding after the war in leading scientific journals. See Heinrich Kraut, "Calorie Intake and Industrial Output," *Science* 104 (1946): 496–97, and "Triglyceride Fats in Human Nutrition: Physiological Value of Synthetic Fats," *British Journal of Nutrition* 3 (1949): 355–58. He was one of the founders of the Deutsche Gesellschaft für Ernährung after the war and received the *Bundesverdienstkreuz* in 1963.

34. Rudolf Höss, *Commandant of Auschwitz: The Autobiography of Rudolf Höss* (Cleveland: World Publishing, 1959), 230.

35. Heim, *Kalorien*, 133.

36. Zięba, "Das Nebenlager Rajsko," 86.

37. Wieland, *Die politischen Aufgaben*, 51.

38. Bernhard Strebel and Jens-Christian Wagner, "No Time to Debate and Ask Questions: Forced Labor for Science in the Kaiser Wilhelm Society, 1939–1945," in Heim, *The Kaiser Wilhelm Society under National Socialism*, 47–73.

39. See note 34.

40. The relationship between Nazism and nature conservation was first discussed at a conference in Berlin "Naturschutz and Nationalsozialismus," in 2002. See the volume edited by Joachim Radkau and Frank Uekötter, *Naturschutz und Nationalsozialismus* (Frankfurt: Campus Verlag, 2003). See also Franz-Josef Brüggemeier, Mark Cioc, and Thomas Zeller, eds., *How Green Were the Nazis? Nature, Environment, and Nation in the Third Reich* (Athens: Ohio University Press, 2005).

41. Göring has been called the "father of the national conservation law." See Frank Uekötter, *The Green and the Brown: A History of Conservation in Nazi Germany* (Cambridge: Cambridge University Press, 2006), 69.

42. Himmler in his speech to SS leaders in Posen on October 4, 1943. Here quoted from Uekötter, *The Green and the Brown*, 57.

43. Uekötter, *The Green and the Brown*, 63.

44. Uekötter, *The Green and the Brown*, 74.

45. Uekötter, *The Green and the Brown*, 70.

46. Michael Imort, "Eternal Forest—Eternal Volk. The Rhetoric and Reality of National Socialist Forest Policy," in Brüggemeier, *How Green Were the Nazis?*, 43–72.

47. Uekötter, *The Green and the Brown*, 71.

48. See Thomas Zeller, "Molding the Landscape of Nazi Environmentalism. Alwin Seifert and the Third Reich," in Brueggemeier, *How Green Were the Nazis?* 147–70.

49. The argument was first brought up by Anna Bramwell, *Blood and Soil: Walther Darré and Hitler's "Green Party"* (Abbotsbrook: Bourne End, 1985). More recently, other authors have claimed that there is a connection between today's green movements and Nazism. See Janet Biehl and Peter Staudenmaier, *Ecofascism: Lessons from the German Experience* (Edinburgh: AK Press, 1995).

50. See, for example, Radkau and Uekötter, *Naturschutz and Nationalsozialismus*, Radkau and Uekötter, *The Green and the Brown.*

51. Gesine Gerhard, "Richard Walther Darré—Naturschützer oder 'Rassenzüchter'?" in Radkau and Uekötter, *Naturschutz and Nationalsozialismus*, 257–72.

52. See Gesine Gerhard, "Breeding Pigs and People for the Third Reich: Richard Walther Darré's Agrarian Ideology," in Brüggemeier, *How Green Were the Nazis?*, 129–48.

53. Gerhard, *Richard Walther Darré*, 261.

54. On Darré's ideology and political career, see Gerhard, "Breeding Pigs," and Gesine Gerhard, "Food and Genocide: Nazi Agrarian Food Policy in the Occupied Territories of the Soviet Union," *Contemporary European History* 18, no. 1 (2009): 45–65.

55. Uwe Werner, *Anthroposophen in der Zeit des Nationalsozialismus* (Oldenbourg: Wissenschaftsverlag, 1999), 89ff.

56. Diary Darré, November 10, 1937, BAK N 1094 I, 65a, fol. 63. See Gerhard, *Richard Walther Darré*, 263.

57. Darré, June 7, 1941, BAK NS 19/3122, fol. 67–72.

58. Darré, June 16, 1941, BAK NS 19/3122, fol. 54. See Gerhard, *Richard Walther Darré*, 265–67.

59. Gerhard, "Food and Genocide," 266–67.

60. In postwar literature, some took Darré's interest in alternative farming methods and described him as an "early green." This characterization promoted by Anna Bramwell in her book has been sharply criticized by other historians, but her argument continues to be used. For a critical review of Bramwell's thesis see Gerhard, *Richard Walther Darré*, and Uekötter, *The Green and the Brown*.

61. Here quoted from Uekötter, *The Green and the Brown*, 30. Uekötter comes to the conclusion that Hitler's own sense for the beauty of nature was very limited.

62. Rynn Berry, *Hitler: Neither Vegetarian nor Animal Lover* (New York: Pythagorean Publishers, 2004), and Biehl and Staudenmeier, *Ecofascism*.

63. Lizzie Collingham, *The Taste of War: World War II and the Battle for Food* (New York: Penguin Press, 2011), 355ff.

64. Berry, *Hitler*, 30.

65. Berry, *Hitler*, 39.

66. Some writers seem to think so. See, for example, Martin Rowe in his introduction to Rynn Berry, *Hitler: Neither Vegetarian nor Animal Lover* (New York: Pythoagorean Publisher, 2004).

6. THE HUNGER YEARS AFTER THE WAR

1. Here quoted from Gustavo Corni and Horst Gies, *Brot—Butter—Kanonen. Die Ernährungswirtschaft in Deutschland unter der Diktatur Hitlers* (Berlin: Akademie Verlag, 1997), 576.

2. Corni and Gies, *Brot—Butter—Kanonen*, 577.

3. Corni and Gies, *Brot—Butter—Kanonen*, 577.

4. See Gesine Gerhard, "Food and Genocide: Nazi Agrarian Food Policy in the Occupied Territories of the Soviet Union," *Contemporary European History* 18, no. 1 (2009): 45–65.

5. Letter to Ursula Backe, August 21, 1942, BAL N 1075, no. 1. See also Gerhard, "Food and Genocide," 62–63.

6. Letter to his wife from October 2, 1944, in BAK N 1075, no. 1.

7. Letter to Ursula from August 29, 1944, BAK N 1075, no. 1.

8. Gerhard, "Food and Genocide," 63.

9. Letter to Ursula from February 4, 1945, BAK N 1075, no. 1.

10. See letters from November 23, 1944, February 4, 1945, and August 2, 1943, BAK N 1075, no. 1. See also Ursula Backe's diary entry on August 7, 1944, BAK N 1075, no. 19.

11. Letter to Ursula from November 13, 1944, BAK N 1075, no. 1.

12. Both documents are in the Federal Archives, NL Backe.

13. See Backe's letter to his wife from January 31, 1946, p. 9, BAK N 1075, no. 1.

14. Letter to his wife from January 31, 1946, pp. 8–9, BAK N 1075, no. 1. He called the letter a "draft of a testament" and explained his political motivations and ideas. See also Backe, *Grosser Bericht.*

15. Paul Körner had been a state secretary in the Four-Year Plan administration and was involved in the planning for the starvation of the Soviet Union.

16. Conversation with Armgard Henning née Backe, Albrecht Backe, and Arndt Backe on June 2, 2004, in Hanover.

17. Ursula Backe's diaries say little about Herbert's death. There are only few diary entries from this time period. See BAK NL 1075, nos. 21 and 22. The last letter Ursula received from Herbert was written on March 28, 1947. She did not seem to know about her husband's suicide plans or his motives. Backe probably feared that the Nuremberg judges would condemn his food policies. During the interrogation, Robert Kempner had confronted him with evidence of the "hunger plan." See the notes of the interrogation in BAK N 1470 Robert Kempner, no. 523. Conversation with Backe's children on June 2, 2004. See also Gerhard, "Food and Genocide," 64.

18. Anna Bramwell mentioned Backe in her study of Darré, see Anna Bramwell, *Blood and Soil: Richard Walther Darré and Hitler's "Green Party"* (Abbotsbrook: Bourne End, 1985). See also Joachim Lehmann, "Herbert Backe—Technokrat und Agrarideologe," in *Die Braune Elite II. 21 Weitere biographische Skizzen*, eds. Ronald Smelzer, Enrico Syring, and Rainer Zitelmann (Darmstadt: Wissenschaftliche Buchgesellschaft, 1993), 1–12. See also Bertold Alleweldt, "Herbert Backe—Eine politische Biographie" (master's thesis, Johann Wolfgang Goethe-Universität, 2000; published as a book by Wissenschaftlicher Verlag in 2011). See the critical examinations of Backe by Corni and Gies, *Brot—Butter—Kanonen*, and Susanne Heim, *Kalorien, Kautschuk, Karrieren. Pflanzenzüchtung und Landwirtschaftliche Forschung in Kaiser-Wilhelm-Instituten, 1933–1945* (Göttingen: Wallstein Verlag, 2003).

19. Darré had to give up his office in Berlin and begged Backe to let him keep at least a secretary. See Darré's letter from January 26, 1943, BAK R 43 II, no. 657.

20. Darré's (edited) diaries do not have any entries between March 1941 and October 1943. According to his long-time confident Hans Deetjen, who edited the diaries in 1969 and burned the originals, Darré did not keep a diary during that time because of the difficulties of his political dismissal. See his explanation in the edited diaries the City Archives in Goslar, NL Darré, no. 484. Deetjen's depiction of Darré is apologetic and it can be assumed that he edited the diaries in order to free Darré from any responsibility for the Nazi crimes. The diaries cannot be considered a reliable source. See Gerhard, "Food and Genocide," 64.

21. Benz, *Riecke*, 79.

22. See Institut für Zeitgeschichte (IfZ) ED 110, no. 3, 561–70.

23. See Lehmann, "Herbert Backe," Corni and Gies, *Brot—Butter—Kanonen*, Heim, *Kalorien, Kautschuk, Karrieren* and Gerhard, "Food and Genocide."

24. Bramwell, *Blood and Soil*, 188; Gerhard, *Breeding Pigs*, 140.

25. Darré was buried in Goslar, the city the Nazis had declared to be the "Reichsbauernhaupstadt." The city archives in Goslar hold the personal papers of Richard Walther Darré.

26. Benz, *Riecke*, 74.

27. Alfred Rosenberg (1893–1946) was the chief Nazi ideologist and Minister of the Eastern Occupied Territories.

28. Here quoted from Benz, *Riecke*, 77.

29. Here quoted from Benz, *Riecke*, 77.

30. Corni and Gies, *Brot—Butter—Kanonen*, 581–82.

31. Rainer Gries, *Die Rationen-Gesellschaft. Versorgungskampf und Vergleichsmentalität. Leipzig, München und Köln nach dem Kriege* (Münster: Verlag Westfälisches Dampfboot, 1991), 26–27.

32. www.dw.de/care-packages-prevented-starvation-in-post-war-germany/a-15313828 (accessed October 22, 2014).

33. Hermann Graml, *Die Alliierten und die Teilung Deutschlands. Konflikte und Entscheidungen, 1941–1948* (Frankfurt: Fischer Taschenbuch Verlag), 1985.

34. On the economic situation in postwar Germany, see Alan Kramer, *The West German Economy, 1945–1955* (New York: Berg Publisher, 1991). See also Günter Trittel, *Hunger und Politik. Die Ernährungskrise in der Bizone (1945–1949)* (Frankfurt: Campus Verlag, 1990), Paul Erker, *Ernährungskrise und Nachkriegsgesellschaft*, and John E. Farquharson, *The Western Allies and the Politics of Food: Agrarian Management in Postwar Germany* (Oxford: Berg Publishers), 1985.

35. See Gesine Gerhard, *Peasants into Farmers: Agriculture and Democracy in West Germany* (dissertation thesis, University of Iowa, 2000), 69.

36. See Gerhard, *Peasants into Farmers*, 59–71.

37. James Edward Smith, ed., *The Papers of General Lucius D. Clay*, vol. 1 (Bloomington: Indiana University Press, 1974), 184.

38. Here quoted from Gerhard, *Peasants into Farmers*, 71.

39. N. M. Nairmark, *The Russians in Germany: A History of the Soviet Zone of Occupation, 1945–1949* (Cambridge, MA: Belknap Press of Harvard University Press, 1995).

40. On the land reform see Gregory W. Sandford, *From Hitler to Ulbricht: The Communist Reconstruction of East Germany, 1945–46* (Princeton, NJ: Princeton University Press, 1983); Martin McCauley, *The German Democratic Republic since 1945* (London: Macmillan, 1983); and J. P. Nettl, *The Eastern Zone and Soviet Policy in Germany, 1945–1950* (London: Oxford University Press, 1951). See also Arnd Bauernkämper, "Von der Bodenreform zur Kollektivierung. Zum Wandel der ländlichen Gesellschaft in der Sowjetischen Besatzungszone Deutschlands und DDR, 1945–1952," in *Sozialgeschichte der DDR*, eds. Hartmut Kaelble, Jürge Kocka, and Harmut Zwahr (Stuttgart: Klett Cotta, 1994), 119–43.

41. Nettl, *The Eastern Zone and Soviet Policy*, 176–77.

42. See Antonia Maria Humm, *Auf dem Weg zum Sozialistischen Dorf? Zum Wandel der dörflichen Lebenswelt in der DDR und der Bundesrepublik Deutschland, 1952–1969* (Göttingen: Vandenhoeck & Ruprecht, 1999).

43. Gerhard, *Peasants into Farmers*, 78–79.

44. Humm, *Auf dem Weg zum Sozialistischen Dorf?*, 89.

45. Humm, *Auf dem Weg zum Sozialistischen Dorf?*, 114.

46. Gerhard, *Peasants into Farmers*, 80, 123–24. See also Arnd Bauerkämper, "Zwangsmodernisierung unf Krisenzyklen. Die Bodenreform und

Kollektivierung in Brandenburg 1945–1960/61," *Geschichte und Gesellschaft* 25, no. 4 (1999): 556–88, 577.

47. On food distribution in the occupied zones see Gries, *Die Rationen-Gesellschaft*.

48. Hermann Dietrich (1879–1954) was Reichsminister of Food and Agriculture from 1928–1930 and Reichsminister of Finance from 1930–1932.

49. Hanse Schlange was born in 1866 on the estate Schöningen in the Eastern province of Pomerania. After he fled the advancing Red Army troops to the West, he added the name of his family's estate to his name. He was one of the cofounders of the conservative party Christian Democratic Union (*Christlich Demokratische Union*, CDU) in 1945 and as the man in charge of food policy from 1945 to 1948 probably one of the best-known politicians. His name has been largely forgotten. His personal papers are in the Bundesarchiv in Koblenz, Germany.

50. See Gerhard, *Peasants into Farmers*, 88–90.

51. Justus Rohrbach, *Im Schatten des Hungers. Dokumentarisches zur Ernährungspolitik und Ernährungswirtschaft in den Jahren, 1945–1948* (Hamburg: Paul Parey, 1955).

52. Gerhard, *Peasants into Farmers*, 98–99.

53. Here quoted from Trittel, *Hunger und Politik*, 116. See Gerhard, *Peasants into Farmers*, 85.

54. Quoted from Wolfgang Benz, *Von der Besatzungsherrschaft zur Bundesrepublik, Stationen einer Staatsgründung, 1946–1949* (Frankfurt: Fischer Taschenbuch Verlag, 1989). See also Gerhard, *Peasants into Farmers*, 102.

55. James K. Pollock (1898–1968) was a political scientist at the University of Michigan and served as a personal advisor to Military Governor Clay in the Western zones of occupation.

56. Erker, *Ernährungskrise*, 246, and Gerhard, *Peasants into Farmers*, 112ff.

57. Gerhard, *Peasants into Farmers*, 114.

58. David R. Henderson, "The German Economic Miracle." *Concise Encyclopedia of Economics* (accessed December 12, 2014), www.econlib.org/library/Enc/GermanEconomicMiracle.html.

59. Gesine Gerhard, "Das Ende der deutschen Bauernfrage: Ländliche Gesellschaft im Umbruch," in *Der lange Abschied vom Agrarland. Agrarpolitik, Landwirtschaft und ländliche Gesellschaft zwischen Weimar und Bonn*, ed. Daniela Münkel (Göttingen: Wallstein-Verlag, 2000), 124–42.

60. Ursula Heinzelmann, *Food Culture in Germany* (Westport, CT: Greenwood Press, 2008), 29.

61. Wolfgang Protzner, ed., *Vom Hungerwinter zum kulinarischen Schlaraffenland. Aspekte einer Kulturgeschichte des Essens in der Bundesrepublik Deutschland* (Wiesbaden: Franz Steiner Verlag), 1987.

62. On the changes in food habits see Michael Wildt, *Am Beginn der "Konsumgesellschaft." Mangelerfahrung, Lebenshaltung, Wohlstandshoffnung in Westdeutschland in den fünfziger Jahren* (Hamburg: Ergebnisse Verlag, 1994), and Arne Anderson, *Der Traum vom guten Leben: Alltags-und Konsumgeschichte vom Wirtschaftswunder bis heute* (Frankfurt: Campus Verlag, 1997).

63. Alan Milward, *The European Rescue of the Nation-State* (London: Routledge, 2000), and Rosemary Fennell, *The Common Agricultural Policy: Continuity and Change* (Oxford: Clarendon Press, 1997).

64. The EEC was the forerunner to the European Community and the European Union established by the Maastricht Treaty in 1993.

65. Gerhard, *Peasants into Farmers*, 190.

66. Gerhard, *Peasants into Farmers*, 213.

SELECTED BIBLIOGRAPHY AND SOURCES

PRIMARY SOURCES AND ARCHIVAL COLLECTIONS

Bundesarchiv Berlin, Germany (BAB)

NS 2 *Rasse-und Siedlungshauptamt* (RuSHA, Race and Settlement Office).
R 16 *Reichs-Nährstand* (RNS, Reich Food Estate).
R 3601 *Reichsministerium für Ernährung und Landwirtschaft* (RMEL, Reich Ministry of Food and Agriculture).

Bundesarchiv Koblenz, Germany (BAK)

NL 1094 II Richard Walther Darré.
NL 1075 Herbert Backe.

Stadtarchiv Goslar, Germany (SAG)

NL Richard Walther Darré.
Backe, Herbert. *Um die Nahrungsfreiheit Europas. Weltwirtschaft oder Großraum*, 2nd. ed. Leipzig: Wilhelm Goldmann Verlag, 1943.
Backe, Herbert. *Volk und Wirtschaft im national-sozialistischen Deutschland. Reden des Staatssekretärs im Reichs- und Preussischen Ministerium für Ernährung und Landwirtschaft*. Berlin: Reichsnährstandsverlag, o.J.
Darré, Richard Walther. *Das Bauerntum als Lebensquell der nordischen Rasse*, 4th ed. München: Lehmann, 1934.
———. *Um Blut und Boden. Reden und Aufsätze*, 4th ed. München: Zentralverlag der NSDAP, 1942.
Höss, Rudolf. *Commandant of Auschwitz: The Autobiography of Rudolf Höss.* Cleveland, OH: World Publishing, 1959.

SELECTED BIBLIOGRAPHY

Alexander, Jennifer. "An Efficiency of Scarcity: Using Food to Increase the Productivity of Soviet Prisoners of War in the Mines of the Third Reich." *History and Technology* 4, no. 22 (2006): 391–406.

Aly, Götz, and Susanne Heim. *Vordenker der Vernichtung. Auschwitz und die deutschen Pläne für eine neue europäische Ordnung*, 2nd ed. Frankfurt: Fischer Taschenbuch Verlag, 1993.

Alleweldt, Bertold. *Herbert Backe—Eine politische Biographie.* Berlin: Wissenschaftlicher Verlag, 2011.

Anderson, Arne. *Der Traum vom guten Leben: Alltags-und Konsumgeschichte vom Wirtschaftswunder bis heute.* Frankfurt: Campus Verlag, 1997.

Baten, Jörg, and Andrea Wagner. "Autarchy, Market Disintegration, and Health: The Mortality and Nutritional Crisis in Nazi Germany, 1933–1937." *Economics and Human Biology* 1 (2002): 1–28.

Bauernkämper, Arnd. "Agrarwirtschaft und ländliche Gesellschaft in der Bundesrepublik Deutschland und der DDR. Eine Bilanz der Jahre, 1945–1965," *Aus Politik und Zeitgeschichte* B 38/97 (1997): 25–37.

———. "Zwangsmodernisierung und Krisenzyklen. Die Bodenreform und Kollektivierung in Brandenburg, 1945–1960/61." *Geschichte und Gesellschaft* 25, no. 4 (1999): 556–88.

Benz, Wigbert. *Hans-Joachim Riecke, NS-Staatsekretär. Vom Hungerplaner vor, zum "Welternährer" nach 1945.* Berlin: Wissenschaftlicher Verlag, 2014.

———. *Der Hungerplan im "Unternehmen Barbarossa," 1941.* Berlin: Wissenschaftlicher Verlag, 2011.

Benz, Wolfgang. *Von der Besatzungsherrschaft zur Bundesrepublik, Stationen einer Staatsgründung, 1946–1949.* Frankfurt: Fischer Taschenbuch Verlag, 1989.

Bergmann, Jürgen, and Klaus Megerle. "Protest und Aufruhr der Landwirtschaft in der Weimarer Republik (1924–1933). Formen und Typen der politischen Agrarbewegung im regionalen Vergleich." In *Regionen im historischen Vergleich. Studien zu Deutschland im 19. und 20. Jahrhundert*, edited by J. Bergmann et al., 201–87. Opladen: Westdeutscher Verlag, 1989.

Bergmann, Klaus. *Agrarromantik und Grosstadtfeindschaft.* Meisenheim a. Glan: Hain, 1970.

Berkhoff, K. C. *Harvest of Despair: Life and Death in Ukraine under Nazi Rule.* Cambridge, MA: Belknap Press of Harvard University Press, 2004.

Bramwell, Anna. *Blood and Soil: Richard Walther Darré and Hitler's "Green Party."* Abbotsbrook: Kensal Press, 1985.

Breitmann, Richard. *The Architect of Genocide: Himmler and the Final Solution.* New York: Knopf, 1991.

Brüggemeier, Franz-Josef, Mark Cioc, and Thomas Zeller, eds. *How Green Were the Nazis? Nature, Environment, and Nation in the Third Reich.* Athens: Ohio University Press, 2005.

Collingham, Lizzie. *The Taste of War: World War I and the Battle for Food.* New York: Penguin Press, 2012.

Corni, Gustavo, and Horst Gies. *Brot—Butter—Kanonen. Die Ernährungswirtschaft in Deutschland unter der Diktatur Hitlers.* Berlin: Akademie Verlag, 1997.

Corni, Gustavo. *Hitler and the Peasants: Agrarian Policy of the Third Reich, 1930–1939.* New York: Berg, 1990.

Davis, Belinda. *Home Fires Burning: Food, Politics and Everyday Life in World War I Berlin.* Chapel Hill: University of North Carolina Press, 2000.

De Lissa, Nelli. *War-Rime Cookery.* Simpkon and Marshall, 1915. Reprinted in *World War I and European Society: A Sourcebook*, edited by Marilyn Shevin-Coetzee and Franz Coetzee. Lexington: D.C. Heath and Company, 1995, 148.

Deichmann, Ute. *Biologen unter Hitler. Porträt einer Wissenschaft im NS-Staat.* Frankfurt: Fischer Taschenbuch Verlag, 1995.

Eichholtz, Dietrich. "Die 'Krautaktion.' Ruhrindustrie, Ernährungswissenschaft und Zwangsarbeit, 1944." In *Europa und der 'Reichseinsatz.' Ausländische Zivilarbeiter, Kriegsgefangene und KZ-Häftlinge in Deutschland, 1938–1945*, edited by Ulrich Herbert, 270–94. Essen: Klartext Verlag, 1991.

Eidenbenz, Mathias. *"Blut und Boden": Zur Funktion und Genese der Metaphern des Agrarismus und Biologismus in der nationalsozialistischen Bauernpropaganda R. W. Darrés*. Bern: Peter Lang, 1993.

Erker, Paul. *Ernährungskrise und Nachkriegsgesellschaft. Bauern und Arbeiterschaft in Bayern, 1943–1953*. Stuttgart: Klett Verlag, 1990.

Flachowsky, Sören. *Von der Notgemeinschaft zum Reichsforschungsrat: Wissenschaftspolitik im Kontext von Autarkie, Aufrüstung, und Krieg*. Stuttgart: Franz Steiner, 2008.

Farquharson, John E. "The Agrarian Policy of National Socialist Germany." In *Peasants and Lords in Modern Germany: Recent Studies in Agricultural History*, edited by Robert G. Moeller, 233–59. Boston: Allen & Unwin, 1986.

———. *The Western Allies and the Politics of Food: Agrarian Management in Postwar Germany*. Oxford: Berg Publishers, 1985.

Fest, Joachim. *Speer: The Final Verdict*. New York: Harcourt, 2001.

Friedlander, Henry. *The Origins of Nazi Genocide: From Euthanasia to the Final Solution*. Chapel Hill: University of North Carolina Press, 1995.

Fullbrook, Mary. *A Small Town Near Auschwitz: Ordinary Nazis and the Holocaust*. Oxford: Oxford University Press, 2012.

Gausemeier, Bernd. *Natürliche Ordnungen und politische Allianzen. Biologische und biochemische Forschung an Kaiser-Wilhelm-Instituten, 1933–1945*. Göttingen: Wallstein Verlag, 2005.

Gelderblom, Bernhard. "Bückeberg." Accessed November 22, 2014. www.gelderblom-hameln.de/bückeberg/bückeberg.html.

Gerhard, Gesine. "Bauernbewegung und Agrarromantik in der Weimarer Republik. Die Bauernhochschulbewegung und die Blut-und-Boden-Ideologie des Nationalsozialismus." M.A. thesis, Technische Universität Berlin, 1994.

———. "Breeding Pigs and People for the Third Reich: Richard Walter Darré's Agrarian Ideology." In *How Green Were the Nazis? Nature, Environment, and Nation in the Third Reich*, ed. by Franz-Josef Brüggemeier, Marc Cioc, and Thomas Zeller, 129–46. Athens: Ohio University Press, 2005.

———. "Food and Genocide: Nazi Agrarian Food Policy in the Occupied Territories of the Soviet Union." *Contemporary European History* 18, no. 1 (2009): 45–65.

———. "Food as a Weapon: Agricultural Sciences and the Building of a Greater German Empire." *Food, Culture and Society* 14, no. 3 (2011): 335–51.

———. "Das Ende der deutschen Bauernfrage: Ländliche Gesellschaft im Umbruch." In *Der lange Abschied vom Agrarland. Agrarpolitik, Landwirtschaft und ländliche Gesellschaft zwischen Weimar und Bonn*, edited by Daniela Münkel, 124–42. Göttingen: Wallstein-Verlag, 2000.

———. "Peasants into Farmers: Agriculture and Democracy in West Germany." PhD dissertation, University of Iowa, 2000.

Gerlach, Christian. *Kalkulierte Morde. Die deutsche Wirtschafts- und Vernichtungspolitik in Weißrussland 1941 bis 1944*. Hamburg: HIS Verlag, 1998.

———. *Krieg, Ernährung, Völkermord. Deutsche Vernichtungspolitik im Zweiten Weltkrieg*. Zürich: Pendo Verlag, 2001.

Gies, Horst. "Die nationalsozialistische Machtergreifung auf dem agrarpolitischen Sektor." *Zeitschrift für Agrargeschichte und Agrarsoziologie*, vol. 16 (1967): 210–32.

———. "The NSDAP and Agrarian Organizations in the Final Phase of the Weimar Republic." In *Nazism and the Third Reich*, edited by H. A. Turner, 45–88. New York: Quadrangle Books, 1972.

Graml, Hermann. *Die Alliierten und die Teilung Deutschlands. Konflikte und Entscheidungen, 1941–1948*. Frankfurt: Fischer Taschenbuch Verlag, 1985.

Grando, Stefano, and Gianluca Volpi. "Backwardness, Modernization, Propaganda: Agrarian Policies and Rural Representations in the Italian Fascist Regime." In *Agriculture in the Age of Fascism: Authoritarian Technocracy and Rural Modernization, 1922–1945*, edited by Lourenzo Fernández-Prieto, Juan Pan-Montojo, and Miguel Cabo, 43–84. Turnboat, Belgium: Brepols, 2014.

Gries, Rainer. *Die Rationen-Gesellschaft. Versorgungskampf und Vergleichsmentalität. Leipzig, München und Köln nach dem Kriege.* Münster: Verlag Westfälisches Dampfboot, 1991.
Grundmann, Friedrich. *Agrarpolitik im 3. Reich. Anspruch und Wirklichkeit des Reichserbhofgesetzes.* Hamburg: Hoffmann und Campe, 1979.
Heim, Susanne, ed. *Autarkie und Ostexpansion. Pflanzenzucht und Agrarforschung im Nationalsozialismus.* Göttingen: Wallstein Verlag, 2002.
———. *Kalorien, Kautschuk, Karrieren. Pflanzenzüchtung und landwirtschaftliche Forschung in Kaiser-Wilhelm-Instituten, 1933–1945.* Göttingen: Wallstein Verlag, 2003.
Heim, Susanne, Carola Sachse, and Mark Walker, eds. *The Kaiser Wilhelm Society under National Socialism.* New York: Cambridge University Press, 2009.
Heinzelmann, Ursula. *Food Culture in Germany.* Westport, CT: Greenwood Press, 2008.
Herbert, Ulrich. *Europa und der "Reichseinsatz." Ausländische Zivilarbeiter, Kriegsgefangene und KZ-Häftlinge in Deutschland, 1938–1945.* Essen: Klartext Verlag, 1991.
Hügel, Arnulf. *Kriegsernährungswirtschaft Deutschlands während des Ersten und Zweiten Weltkriegs.* Konstanz: Hartung-Gorre-Verlag, 2003.
Humm, Antonia. *Auf dem Weg zum sozialistischen Dorf? Zum Wandel der dörflichen Lebenswelt in der DDR und der Bundesrepublik Deutschland, 1952–1969.* Göttingen: Vandenhoeck & Ruprecht, 1999.
Jones, Larry Eugene. "Crisis and Realignment: Agrarian Splinter Parties in the Late Weimar Republic, 1928–1933." In *Peasants and Lords in Modern Germany: Recent Studies in Agricultural History*, edited by Robert G. Moeller, 198–232. Boston: Allen & Unwin, 1986.
Kay, Alex J. *Exploitation, Resettlement, Mass Murder: Political and Economic Planning for German Occupation Policy in the Soviet Union, 1940–1941.* New York: Berghahn Books, 2006.
———. "Germany's Staatssekretäre, Mass Starvation and the Meeting of May 2, 1941." *Journal of Contemporary History* 41, no. 4 (2006): 685–700.
———. "The Purpose of the Russian Campaign Is the Decimation of the Slavic Population by Thirty Million: The Radicalization of German Food Policy in Early 1941." In *Nazi Policy on the Eastern Front, 1941: Total War, Genocide, and Radicalization,* edited by Alex J. Kay, Jeff Rutherford, and David Stahel, 101–29. Rochester, NY: University of Rochester Press, 2012.
Kinzler, Sonja. *Kanonen statt Butter. Ernährung und Propaganda im "Dritten Reich."* Exhibition catalog, Kiel, 2006.
Köstlin, Konrad. "Der Eintopf der Deutschen. Das Zusammengekochte als Kultessen." In *Tübinger Beitrage zur Volkskultur*, edited by Utz Jeggle et al., 220–41. Tübingen: Gulde-Druck, 1986.
Kramer, Alan. *The West German Economy, 1945–1955.* New York: Berg Publishers, 1991.
Langthaler, Ernst. "Agrar-Europa unter Nationalsozialistischen Vorzeichen (1933–1945)." *Themenportal Europäische Geschichte*, www.euopa.clio-online.de, June 19, 2011.
Lehmann, Joachim. "Herbert Backe—Technokrat und Agrarideologe." In *Die Braune Elite II. 21 Weitere Biographische Skizzen*, edited by Ronald Smelzer, Enrico Syring, and Rainer Zitelmann, 1–12. Darmstadt: Wissenschaftliche Buchgesellschaft, 1993.
Lifton, Robert. *The Nazi Doctors: Medical Killing and the Psychology of Genocide.* New York: Basic Books, 2000.
Lummel, Peter. "Food Provisioning in the German Army of the First World War." In *Food and War in Twentieth Century Europe*, edited by Ina Zweininger, Rachel Duffett, and Alain Drouard, 13–25. Surrey, England: Ashgate, 2001.
Macrakis, Kristie. *Surviving the Swastika: Scientific Research in Nazi Germany.* New York: Oxford University Press, 1993.
Moeller, Robert G. *War Stories: The Search for a Usable Past in the Federal Republic of Germany.* Berkeley: University of California Press, 2001.
Müller, Rolf-Dieter. "Die Konsequenzen der 'Volksgemeinschaft': Ernährung, Ausbeutung und Vernichtung." In *Der Zweite Weltkrieg. Analysen—Grundzüge—Forschungsbilanz*, edited by Wolfgang Michalka, 240–49. Weyarn: Seehamer Verlag, 1989, 1997.
Müller-Hill, Benno. *Murderous Science: Elimination by Scientific Selection of Jews, Gypsies, and Others in Germany, 1933–1945.* New York: Oxford University Press, 1988.

Nairmark, N. M. *The Russians in Germany: A History of the Soviet Zone of Occupation, 1945–1949.* Cambridge, MA: Belknap Press of Harvard University Press, 1995.

North, Jonathan. "Soviet Prisoners of War: Forgotten Nazi Victims of World War II." *World War II Magazine* January/February 2006. www.historynet.com/soviet-prisoners-of-war-forgotten-nazi-victims-of-world-war-ii.htm.

Pomp, Rainer. *Bauern und Grossgrundbesitzer auf ihrem Weg ins Dritte Reich. Der Brandenburgische Landbund, 1918–1933.* Berlin: Akademie Verlag, 2011.

Protzner, Wolfgang, ed. *Vom Hungerwinter zum kulinarischen Schlaraffenland. Aspekte einer Kulturgeschichte des Essens in der Bundesrepublik Deutschland.* Wiesbaden: Franz Steiner Verlag, 1987.

Radkau, Joachim, and Frank Uekötter, eds. *Naturschutz und Nationalsozialismus.* Frankfurt: Campus Verlag, 2003.

Rohrbach, Justus. *Im Schatten des Hungers. Dokumentarisches zur Ernährungspolitik und Ernährungswirtschaft in den Jahren, 1945–1948.* Hamburg: Paul Parey, 1955.

Rürup, Rainer, ed. *Der Krieg gegen die Sowjetunion, 1941–1945. Eine Dokumentation.* Berlin: Argon Verlag, 1991.

Rürup, Reinhard, and Wolfgang Schieder, eds. *Geschichte der Kaiser-Wilhelm-Gesellschaft im Nationalsozialismus*, 17 vols. Göttingen: Wallstein Verlag, 2000–2007.

Sachse, Carola, ed. *Die Verbindung nach Auschwitz. Biowissenschaften und Menschenversuche an Kaiser-Wilhelm-Instituten. Dokumentation eines Symposiums.* Göttingen: Wallstein Verlag, 2003.

Sawahn, Anke. *Die Frauenlobby vom Land. Die Landfrauenbewegung in Deutschland und ihre Funktionärinnen 1898 bis 1948.* Frankfurt: DLG Verlag, 2009.

Schmuhl, Hans-Walter. "Rasse, Rassenforschung, Rassenpolitik. Annäherung an das Thema." In *Rassenforschung an Kaiser-Wilhelm-Instituten vor und nach 1933*, edited by Hans-Walter Schmuhl. Göttingen: Wallstein Verlag, 2003.

Scriba, Arnulf. "Der 'Kohlrübenwinter' 1916/17." *Lebendiges Museum Online, Deutsches Historisches Museum*, September 8, 2014. Accessed November 22, 2014, www.dhm.de/lemo/html/wk1/kriegsverlauf/steckrue/index.html.

Snyder, Timothy. *Bloodlands: Europe between Hitler and Stalin.* New York: Basic Books, 2010.

Sösemann, Bernd. *Appell unter der Erntekrone. Das Reichserntedankfest in der nationalsozialistischen Diktatur. Jahrbuch für Kommunikationsgeschichte* 2 (2000): 113–56.

Spoerer, Mark, and Jochen Streb. "Guns and Butter—But No Margarine: The Impact of Nazi Agricultural and Consumption Policies on German Food Production and Consumption, 1933–1938." Paper prepared for the XIV International Economic History Congress, 2006.

Stoltenberg, Gerhard. *Politische Strömungen im deutschen Landvolk, 1918–1933. Ein Beitrag zur politischen Meinungsbildung in der Weimarer Republik.* Düsseldorf: Droste Verlag, 1962.

Streit, Christian. *Keine Kameraden. Die Wehrmacht und die sowjetischen Kriegsgefangenen, 1941–1945.* Stuttgart: Deutsche Verlagsanstalt, 1978.

Szöllösi-Janze, Margit. "National Socialism and the Sciences: Reflections, Conclusions and Historical Perspectives." In *Science in the Third Reich*, edited by Margit Szöllösi-Janze, 1–36. Oxford: Berg Publishers, 2001.

Teuteberg, Hans-Jürgen. "Food Provisioning on the German Home Front, 1914–1918." In *Food and War in Twentieth Century Europe*, edited by Ina Zweiniger-Bargielowska, Rachel Duffett, and Alain Drouard, 59–72. Surrey, England: Ashgate, 2011.

Tooze, Adam. *Wages of Destruction: The Making and Breaking of the German Nazi Economy.* New York: Penguin Books, 2008, 539.

Treitel, Corinna. "Nature and the Nazi Diet," *Food and Foodways* 17 (2009): 139–58.

Trittel, Günter. *Hunger und Politik. Die Ernährungskrise in der Bizone (1945–1949).* Frankfurt: Campus Verlag, 1990.

Uekötter, Frank. *The Green and the Brown: A History of Conservation in Nazi Germany.* Cambridge: Cambridge University Press, 2006.

Vom Bruch, Rüdiger, Ulrich Herbert, and Patrick Wagner, eds. *Studien zur Geschichte der Deutschen Forschungsgemeinschaft*, 5 vols. Stuttgart: Steiner Verlag, 2007–2010.

Welch, David. *Germany, Propaganda and Total War*. New Brunswick, NJ: Rutgers University Press, 2000.

Werner, Uwe. *Anthroposophen in der Zeit des Nationalsozialismus*. Oldenbourg: Wissenschaftsverlag, 1999.

Weinberg, Gerhard. *Hitler's Foreign Policy, 1933–1939: The Road to World War II*. New York: Enigma Books, 2010.

Weinreb, Alice. "Matters of Taste: The Politics of Food and Hunger in Divided Germany, 1945–1971." PhD dissertation, University of Michigan, 2009.

Wildt, Michael. *Am Beginn der "Konsumgesellschaft." Mangelerfahrung, Lebenshaltung, Wohlstandshoffnung in Westdeutschland in den fünfziger Jahren.* Hamburg: Ergebnisse Verlag, 1994.

Zięba, Anna. "Das Nebenlager Rajsko." *Hefte von Auschwitz* 9 (1966): 75–108.

INDEX